STRATEGIES for Writers

Level F

Authors

Leslie W. Crawford, Ed.D.
Georgia College & State University

Rebecca Bowers Sipe, Ed.D.
Eastern Michigan University

ZB
Zaner-Bloser

Educational Consultants

Barbara Marinak
Reading Supervisor
Mechanicsburg, PA

Catherine C. Thome, Ed.D.
English/Language Arts and Assessment Coordinator
Educational Services Division
Lake County Regional Office of Education
Grayslake, IL

Science Content Reviewer

Michael Grote, Ed.D.
Math and Science Education
Columbus Public Schools
Columbus, OH

Teacher Reviewers

Janice Andrus, Chanhassen, MN
Shannon Basner, Hollis, NY
Teressa D. Bell, Nashville, TN
Victoria B. Casady, Ferguson, MO
Kristin Cashman, Mechanicsburg, PA
Jeanie Denaro, Brooklyn, NY
Susan H. Friedman, Ph.D., Sharon, PA
Katherine Harrington, Mechanicsburg, PA
Dianna L. Hinderer, Ypsilanti, MI

Eleanor Kane, Stow, OH
Jean Kochevar, Minneapolis, MN
Diane L. Nicholson, Pittsburgh, PA
Susan Peery, San Antonio, TX
David Philpot, San Francisco, CA
Jodi Ramos, San Antonio, TX
Jacqueline Sullivan, Sunnyvale, CA
Rita Warden-Short, Brentwood, TN
Roberta M. Wykoff, Stow, OH

Page Design Concepts and Cover Design

Tommaso Design Group

Photo Credits

Models: George C. Anderson Photography

p17, Craig Tuttle, Corbis Stock Market; p20, Mug Shots, Corbis Stock Market; p27, Shmuel Thaler, Index Stock Imagery; pp33, 83, Corbis Images, PictureQuest; pp41,127, Andre Jenny, Focus Group, PictureQuest; p51, The Farmers' Museum Inc., Cooperstown, NY; p63, C. Borland, PhotoLink, PhotoDisc, PictureQuest; pp66, 85, 86, 89, George C. Anderson Photography; pp75, 76, 77, Laurie E. Naranjo; p84, The Connecticut Historical Society, Hartford, Connecticut; p105, Bob Krist, eStock Photography, PictureQuest; p117, Dynamic Graphics; p141, Mike Dobel, Masterfile Corporation; p147, Scenics of America, PhotoLink, PhotoDisc, PictureQuest; pp148, 151, 159, Dave Robertson, Masterfile Corporation; p167, Jeremy Woodhouse, Getty Images, PhotoDisc; p169, Anson Industries Limited, EWA; p177, Index Stock Imagery, Inc.; p189, Bill Bachmann, Photo Network; pp193, 197, Corbis Images, PictureQuest; p194, Getty Images, Eyewire; p211, Digital Vision, PictureQuest; p215, Dan Gair Photographic, Index Stock Imagery, PictureQuest; p223, Dilip Mehta, Contact Press Images, PictureQuest; p235, Stephen Webster, Worldwide Hideout, Inc.

Art Credits

pp27, 28, 29, 161, 165, 172, 178, Sandy Joncas; p65, Bill Ogden; p224, Rita Enos-Castaldini; HB7, HB8, HB9, HB11, HB24, HB25, HB42, Marilyn Rodgers Bahney Paselsky; HB12, Brooke Albrecht; HB16, Pat DeWitt Grush.

Production, Photo Research, and Art Buying by Laurel Tech Integrated Publishing Services

NARRATIVE
writing

writing

PERSUASIVE

writing

DESCRIPTIVE

writing

EXPOSITORY writing

writing

Extra Practice

Conventions & Skills

CS 1

Writer's HandBook

HB 1

NARRATIVE

writing

tells a story to the reader.

1

Eyewitness Account

2

Historical Episode

NARRATIVE
writing

Eyewitness Account

In this chapter, you will work with one kind of narrative writing: an **eyewitness account**.

An **eyewitness account** is a true and accurate report of an event observed by the writer.

The story on the next page is an eyewitness account. Read the questions below. Then read the account. Keep these questions in mind as you read.

 **Is the first paragraph clear and interesting?**

 **How well does the writer use the 5 W's (*who, what, when, where,* and *why*) to organize the story?**

 **Does the writer make the story more lively by varying sentence beginnings?**

 **Does the writer use interesting and colorful words to make meanings clear?**

 **Has the writer avoided sentence fragments and run-ons?**

The Great Circus Parade

by Joe (Bongo the Clown) Torelli

Last week I was amazed, astounded, flabbergasted, and stupefied! I, Bongo the Clown, fell under the spell of the Great Circus Parade.

As a professional clown, I had to see the parade. Every July, it winds three miles through downtown Milwaukee, Wisconsin. It features wild animals, dozens of circus wagons and bands, hundreds of horses, and thousands of people in costume—including clowns. From near and far, people come to see the spectacle.

The day I attended was cloudless and bright; a faint breeze floated in from Lake Michigan. A drum troop at the start of the parade stirred up the crowd. Following close behind, young men in knickers pedaled high-wheeled bicycles, and mounted police waved from their saddles. By the time the clown snake charmers arrived, the parade was in full swing.

The clowns were funny, but I was more impressed by the historic circus wagons. Each one showed off a dazzling color scheme. As the wheels turned, yellow and orange webbing between the spokes swirled like sunbursts. Huge draft horses with fancy brass harnesses hauled most of the wagons, some weighing more than a ton.

Magnificent bandwagons carried musicians playing grand old tunes. One bandwagon stood out. Sparkling with gold mermaids and swans, it was like something from a fairy tale.

The cage wagons displayed exotic animals, including a pygmy hippo, a buffalo, and a giraffe. I even saw a liger (a cross between a lion and a tiger).

Most splendid were the tableau wagons. Filled with carved and painted wooden figures, they are historical scenes on wheels. A woman dressed as Cleopatra rode a tableau pulled by camels. A two-headed green dragon roared from the top of a tableau that celebrated the age of knights and castles.

At the end of the parade were lumbering elephants and a steam calliope. Belching out plumes of smoke and hooting old-time melodies, the calliope bid farewell to the satisfied crowd. I smiled all the way home, thinking about those sunburst wheels. I'm still smiling. Maybe I should run off to join the circus parade.

Using a Rubric

A rubric is a tool that lists "what counts" for a piece of writing.

How do you use a rubric? You assign 1, 2, 3, or 4 points to describe how well the author did certain writing tasks.

Remember the questions you read on page 10? Those questions were used to make this rubric.

" Hi! I'm Derek. I'm learning how to write an eyewitness account like the one on page 11. You, too? This rubric can help us. Here's how: Read the questions first. Next, read the scoring information for each question. Then we'll use this rubric to evaluate the account you just read. "

Audience
Is the first paragraph clear and interesting?

Organization
How well does the writer use the 5 W's (*who, what, when, where,* and *why*) to organize the story?

Elaboration
Does the writer make the story more lively by varying sentence beginnings?

Clarification
Does the writer use interesting and colorful words to make meanings clear?

Conventions & Skills
Has the writer avoided sentence fragments and run-ons?

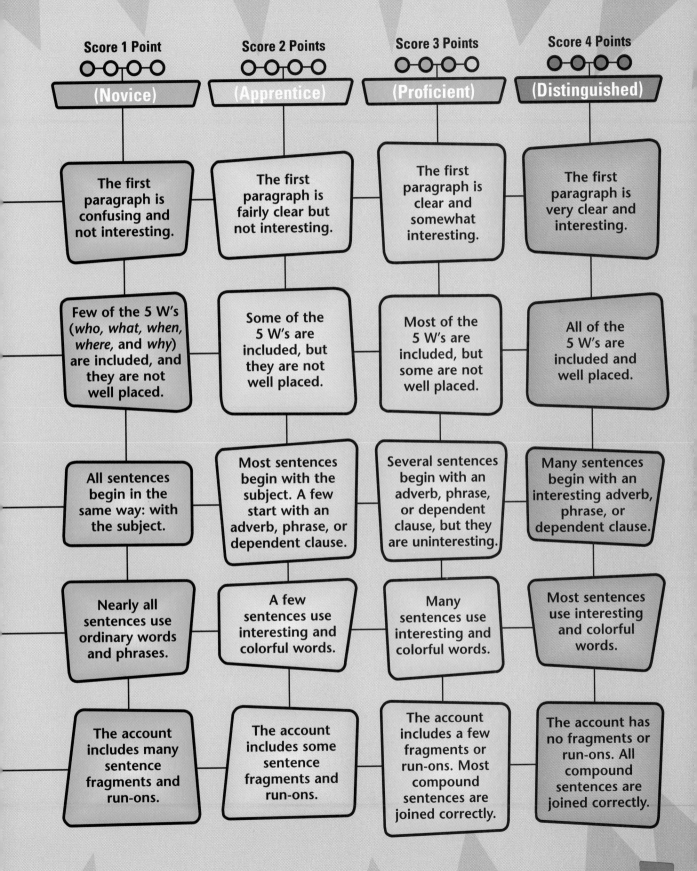

Score 1 Point (Novice)	Score 2 Points (Apprentice)	Score 3 Points (Proficient)	Score 4 Points (Distinguished)
The first paragraph is confusing and not interesting.	The first paragraph is fairly clear but not interesting.	The first paragraph is clear and somewhat interesting.	The first paragraph is very clear and interesting.
Few of the 5 W's (*who, what, when, where,* and *why*) are included, and they are not well placed.	Some of the 5 W's are included, but they are not well placed.	Most of the 5 W's are included, but some are not well placed.	All of the 5 W's are included and well placed.
All sentences begin in the same way: with the subject.	Most sentences begin with the subject. A few start with an adverb, phrase, or dependent clause.	Several sentences begin with an adverb, phrase, or dependent clause, but they are uninteresting.	Many sentences begin with an interesting adverb, phrase, or dependent clause.
Nearly all sentences use ordinary words and phrases.	A few sentences use interesting and colorful words.	Many sentences use interesting and colorful words.	Most sentences use interesting and colorful words.
The account includes many sentence fragments and run-ons.	The account includes some sentence fragments and run-ons.	The account includes a few fragments or run-ons. Most compound sentences are joined correctly.	The account has no fragments or run-ons. All compound sentences are joined correctly.

Using a Rubric
to Study the Model

Discuss each question on the rubric with your classmates. Find words and sentences in the story that help answer each one. Use the rubric to evaluate Joe Torelli's eyewitness account on each question.

 **Audience** — **Is the first paragraph clear and interesting?**

" In the first sentence, the writer uses fun and interesting words, such as **astounded** and **flabbergasted,** to describe his reaction to something cool. You want to read the next sentence to see what it is. You find out that he's going to describe a circus parade—and you're hooked! Read those first two sentences again. "

Last week I was amazed, astounded, flabbergasted, and stupefied! I, Bongo the Clown, fell under the spell of the Great Circus Parade.

Organization

How well does the writer use the 5 W's to organize the story?

66 As you read, you find out more about the parade. In this paragraph, you learn **what** the event was (a circus parade), **who** saw it (the writer), and **when** (July). You find out **why** the writer went to see it (because he's a clown), and also **where** it was (Milwaukee). Then the writer provides more details. See how much information he got in that paragraph? 99

As a professional clown, I had to see the parade. Every July, it winds three miles through downtown Milwaukee, Wisconsin. It features wild animals, dozens of circus wagons and bands, hundreds of horses, and thousands of people in costume—including clowns. From near and far, people come to see the spectacle.

Elaboration

Does the writer make the story more lively by varying sentence beginnings?

66 The writer begins his sentences in several ways, as you can see in this paragraph. The first two sentences begin with the subject, but the third one begins with an interesting phrase that describes a bandwagon. 99

Magnificent bandwagons carried musicians playing grand old tunes. One bandwagon stood out. Sparkling with gold mermaids and swans, it was like something from a fairy tale.

Does the writer use interesting and colorful words to make meanings clear?

" Interesting and colorful words help you picture what's happening. This writer doesn't describe the parade in a boring way, such as saying that smoke came out of the calliope. He makes it more interesting by writing that the calliope belched out plumes of smoke. In his account, the elephants don't just walk, they lumber. "

At the end of the parade were lumbering elephants and a steam calliope. Belching out plumes of smoke and hooting old-time melodies, the calliope bid farewell to the satisfied crowd.

Has the writer avoided sentence fragments and run-ons?

" Every sentence in the account has a subject and a verb. There are no fragments or run-ons. "

" Now it's my turn to write!

I'm going to write an eyewitness account about something that I have seen. I'm going to follow the RUBRIC and the model to help me use good writing strategies. Do you want to see how I do it? Come on, then. "

DeRek

Writer of an Eyewitness Account

Name: Derek

Home: Wyoming

Hobbies: rodeos, raising calves for 4-H, reading westerns

Favorite Western: *Walker's Crossing* by Phyllis Reynolds Naylor

Assignment: eyewitness account

17

Prewriting

Gather

Pick an incident I saw. Take notes on what I saw and heard.

" I live on a ranch and help out with the chores. As a reward, I get to go to the rodeos in Cody, Wyoming.

"When my teacher said we were going to write an eyewitness account, I knew I would write about the Buffalo Bill Cody Stampede Rodeo I saw last summer. I sure remember that one. I sat on my bed, looked at my rodeo posters, and started jotting down notes. "

My Notes on the Cody Stampede Rodeo

- every year on July 1–4, in Cody, Wyoming

- smells like animal sweat and dust

- noisy: announcer, crowd cheering, buzzers, animals banging against fences

- Grand Entry parade: flag colors, 4th of July

- timed events: calf roping, barrel racing—fast cowgirl event

- bulldogging (steer wrestling): invented in early 1900s by Will Pickett, an African American cowboy

- rough stock events: bareback, saddle bronc, bull riding—8 seconds and one hand

- rodeo clowns: protect bull riders from bulls

- pickup men: protect bronc riders from broncs

- winners get prize money and rodeo buckle

Go to page 6 in the **Practice** the Strategy **Notebook!**

Narrative Writing • Eyewitness Account

Prewriting

Organize

Use my notes to make a 5 W's chart.

66 One of the things that counts in writing is organization. I learned that from the **Rubric**. I studied my notes to see what kinds of information I had. Then I created a 5 W's chart. This kind of chart helps me organize the answers to important questions that my audience might ask. 99

5 W's Chart

A **5 W's chart** organizes information by asking and answering the following questions: **What** happened? **Who** was there? **Why** did it happen? **When** did it happen? **Where** did it happen?

What happened?	Buffalo Bill Cody Stampede Rodeo, bronc rider bucked high, bull rider thrown over horns, sharpshooter act
Who was there?	my dad and I, cowboys and cowgirls, crowd, rodeo announcers and judges, clowns, animals, sharpshooter
Why did it happen?	so cowboys and cowgirls can show off their skills and entertain people
When did it happen?	July 1–4 last summer (and annually)
Where did it happen?	Cody, Wyoming

Go to page 8 in the **Practice** the Strategy **Notebook!**

Drafting

Write

Draft my account. Put the most important of the 5 W's in the lead paragraph.

"Okay, I'm ready to start writing. According to the **Rubric**, I should think about my audience. My classmates are my audience for this assignment.

"I'm supposed to include the most important of the 5 W's in the lead paragraph. In this case, that would be **what** happened—the rodeo. **Where** it happened is also important. The rest of the 5 W's should be in the story, too, but they can come later.

"I have to make the lead paragraph interesting for my audience, of course. I think I'll open with the rodeo announcer welcoming everyone. That's it! I'll write my first draft and see how it goes. I'll do my best with spelling and grammar and check for mistakes later. I've got to get writing!"

Lead Paragraph

The **lead paragraph** is the first paragraph of a piece of writing. It introduces the topic and should interest the audience.

lead paragraph → # Ride 'em, Cowboy!

"Welcome, folks! Welcome to the annual Buffalo Bill Cody Stampede Rodeo in Cody, Wyoming!" said the announcer. "Let the grand entry begin!"

~~Me and my dad~~ My dad and I yelled as the cowboys and cowgirls came by wearing colorful western clothes. Some of them wore patriotic colors because the rodeo took place over the Fourth of July.

We ~~have~~ had been to the stampede three times before. Last year we sat in the Buzzard's Roost, the best seats in the arena. I could take in everything from up there. It was dusty and I could smell animal sweat and hear the gates banging and see the cowboys hanging out. It was like a big stable.

Timed events were first on the program. Mainly ropeing and racing against the clock. Calf ropeing shows off ~~some~~ ranching skills. I was watching to learn more about ropeing, I had to feel sorry for the calves. A calf would take off from the shoot. Then suddenly it would be ~~lying~~ on the ground bawling with a ~~string of~~ rope tied in a half-hitch around three legs.

Go to page 10 in the **Practice** the Strategy **Notebook!**

Revising

Elaborate

Make the story more lively by varying sentence beginnings.

" I checked the **Rubric** when I finished my first draft. It said I should begin my sentences in different ways.

"I read my draft again and made some changes. The paragraph below shows how I livened up my account by changing some of the sentence beginnings. "

Varying Sentence Beginnings

Sentences that all begin with the **subject** can become boring. Starting some sentences with an **adverb,** a **phrase,** or a **dependent clause** can make writing more lively and interesting.

Starting with the subject: A bull charged into the arena.
Starting with an adverb: Suddenly, a bull charged into the arena.
Starting with a phrase: Breathing fire, a bull charged into the arena.
Starting with a dependent clause: When the gate opened, a bull charged into the arena.

[2nd DRAFT]

starting with a dependent clause →

starting with a phrase — If I remember correctly,

women

Barrel racing is another timed event. It's the only event for ~~girls~~ in
Racing around three barrels,
this rodeo. The cowgirls spurred their horses ~~around three barrels~~
Skillfully,
in a cloverleaf pattern. They ~~were so skilled that they~~ avoided

knocking down any barrels. ————— starting with an adverb

Go to page 12 in the **Practice** the Strategy **Notebook!**

Revising

Clarify
Replace ordinary words or phrases with more interesting and colorful words.

READ TO MYSELF

"I read my second draft to myself to see how it sounded. It was still a little dull because I had used ordinary words, the kind you read all the time. According to the **Rubric**, I should try to use more interesting and colorful words. I noticed that the model also used colorful words to paint a picture for the audience.

"That's what I did next. Wow! What a difference it made! I improved almost every paragraph. See how I jazzed up this one?"

Ordinary Words and Phrases

Ordinary words and phrases are plain and boring. Their meaning is so general that they do not create a clear picture in the reader's mind. They include words such as *nice, good, big,* and *beautiful.*

[3rd DRAFT]

replaced ordinary words

replaced ordinary words

whooped   paraded past

My dad and I ~~yelled~~ as the cowboys and cowgirls ~~came by~~
decked out in   shirts, hats, belts, boots, and chaps.
~~wearing~~ colorful western ~~clothes~~ Some ~~of them~~ wore ~~patriotic colors~~
red, white, and blue
because the rodeo took place over the Fourth of July.

replaced ordinary words

Go to page 14 in the **Practice** the Strategy **Notebook!**

Editing

Proofread

Watch for sentence fragments. To avoid run-ons, check to see that all compound sentences are joined correctly.

" The  says that I should pay attention to conventions and skills. Of course, I'll check spelling, capitalization, and punctuation. I also need to make sure that every sentence has a subject and a verb and that it begins with a capital letter and ends with the correct punctuation mark.

"I'm going to double-check my compound sentences. If I don't join sentences correctly, they will be hard to read. The reader won't know where one thought ends and another one starts. "

Conventions & Skills

Fragments and Run-ons

A sentence that is missing a subject or a verb is called a **fragment**.
Fragment: Always enjoyed the rodeo. (subject missing)
Fragment: My dad and I to the rodeo. (verb missing)

When you join two sentences as a **compound sentence,** you should put a comma followed by a conjunction between them. You can also join them with a semicolon. Sentences that are not joined correctly are called **run-ons**.
Joined correctly: The buzzer goes off, and then the cowboy dismounts.
Joined correctly: The buzzer goes off; then the cowboy dismounts.
Run-on: The buzzer goes off, then the cowboy dismounts.

Extra Practice
See **Fragments and Run-ons** (CS 2–CS 3) in the back of this book.

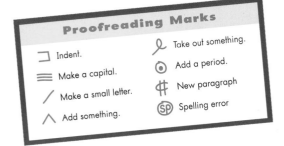

Proofreading Marks

⊐ Indent.

≡ Make a capital.

/ Make a small letter.

∧ Add something.

ℓ Take out something.

⊙ Add a period.

⌗ New paragraph

SP Spelling error

> Here's part of my fourth draft, so you can see the kinds of errors I corrected.

[4th DRAFT]

Rodeo is downright dangerous. Broken bones, cuts and ~~brooses~~ (SP) bruises pulled muscles and concus*hens* (SP) *sions* are common. Riders are trampled. *sometimes*

Cowboys called pickup men protect the bronc rider from the *and* broncs, rodeo clowns protect the bull riders from the bulls. At the

joined compound sentences correctly

stampede, I saw a Brahma *B*ull explode from the ~~shoot~~ (SP) *chute*, twisting like a tornado. The rider flipped over the bull's horns and flopped at its feet. In a flash, a red-nosed rodeo clown distracted the bull ∧and the cowboy sprang up and scrambled over the fence to safety.

made a sentence complete

The stampede always has a famous specialty act. ~~Like~~ a trained *One year, it was* buffalo. Last summer∧it was a sharpshooter who also did tricks with a bullwhip and a lasso. He snapped a target from his own mouth with the whip! Crrrrack! ⌗On the last night, the winners got to take home prize money and a rodeo trophy: a belt buckle⊙I took home a new rodeo poster and a saddlebag of memories.

Go to page 15 in the **Practice** the Strategy **Notebook!**

Publishing

Share Add my account to a class journal.

Writer:	Derek
Assignment:	eyewitness account
Topic:	Buffalo Bill Cody Stampede Rodeo
Audience:	classmates
Method of Publication:	class journal
Reason for Choice:	The class was creating a collection of students' personal experiences.

"Our class was putting together a journal of personal experiences. I decided to put my eyewitness account in the class journal. Here's how I published my story."

1. I checked my story one more time for mistakes.

2. I created a clean copy of my story.

3. I put my title at the top, and below that added "by Derek."

4. I decorated my paper with a rope.

5. I cut out pictures from the rodeo program and added them.

6. I placed my story in the class journal.

Ride 'em, Cowboy!

by Derek

"Welcome, folks! Welcome to the annual Buffalo Bill Cody Stampede Rodeo in Cody, Wyoming!" the announcer's voice blared from the loudspeakers. "Let the Grand Entry begin!"

My dad and I whooped as the cowboys and cowgirls paraded past, decked out in colorful Western shirts, hats, belts, boots, and chaps. Some wore red, white, and blue because the rodeo took place over the Fourth of July.

We had been to the Stampede three times before, but this time we sat in the Buzzard's Roost, the best seats in the arena. From up there, I could take in the entire scene. I could smell animal sweat, hear the gates banging, and see the cowboys hanging out. It was like a big, dusty stable.

First on the program were the timed events, mainly roping and racing against the clock. Calf roping shows off ranching skills. I was watching to learn more about roping, but I had to feel sorry for the calves. One second a calf was running from the chute, and less than 30 seconds later it was on the ground bawling, with a rope tied in a half hitch around three legs.

Barrel racing is another timed event. If I remember correctly, it's the only event for women in this rodeo. Racing around three barrels, the cowgirls spurred their horses in a cloverleaf pattern. Skillfully, they avoided knocking down any barrels.

Almost 100 years ago, an African American cowboy named Will Pickett invented steer wrestling—my favorite timed event. Leaning off the side of his horse, he seized a steer by its horns and slid to the ground. Then he dug in his boot heels and twisted the steer over onto its side. Pickett called it "bulldogging." At the Stampede, the steers were dropping like flies.

Rough stock is the tough stuff: bareback riding, saddle bronc riding, and bull riding. To qualify for the next round in rough stock events, a cowboy has to hang on to a bucking beast with one hand and hold out for at least eight seconds. The first bareback rider flew so high you could see "daylight" between him and the horse. Yee haw! If the rider's free hand touches anything, the judges disqualify him. Then the announcer always remarks, "Let's give him a hand, folks. It may be all he's taking home tonight."

Rodeo is downright dangerous. Broken bones, cuts and bruises, pulled muscles, and concussions are common. Riders are sometimes trampled. Cowboys called "pickup men" protect the bronc riders from the broncs, and rodeo clowns protect the bull riders from the bulls. At the Stampede, I saw a Brahma bull explode from the chute, twisting like a tornado. The rider flipped over the bull's horns and flopped at its feet. In a flash, a red-nosed rodeo clown distracted the bull, and the cowboy sprang up and scrambled over the fence to safety.

The Stampede always has a famous specialty act. One year, it was a trained buffalo. Last summer, it was a sharpshooter who also did tricks with a bullwhip and a lasso. He snapped a target from his own mouth with the whip! Crrrrack!

On the last night, the winners got to take home prize money and a rodeo trophy: a belt buckle. I took home a new rodeo poster and a saddlebag of memories.

USING the Rubric for Assessment

Go to pages 16–17 in the **Practice** the Strategy **Notebook!** Use that rubric to assess Derek's paper. Try using the rubric to assess your own writing.

NARRATIVE writing

Historical Episode

In this chapter, you will work with one kind of narrative writing: **historical episode**.

A **historical episode** is a story that is based on an actual event in history. Both fact and fiction are included and woven together.

The article on the next three pages is a historical episode. Read these questions. Then read the episode, keeping the questions in mind.

 How well does the writer introduce the historic event to the audience?

 Does the story have a clear beginning, middle, and end? Does it stay focused on the event?

 How well does the writer use descriptive details to create a clear picture of the historic period?

 Does the writer put the sentences in a logical order?

 Are quotations punctuated correctly?

CONQUEST OF THE STRATOSPHERE

by Kim Lee

Two men sat across from each other on a train chugging through the Swiss Alps. They had met only an hour earlier, but they were enjoying each other's company. Auguste Piccard, the elder one, was a long-limbed professor. A wreath of wild hair encircled his balding crown. Small round glasses perched on his long slender nose. His mustache wiggled as he talked. Paul Kipfer, the younger man, had sandy hair and soft blue eyes. He didn't talk much. Instead, he listened intently as Auguste described his research on cosmic rays in the atmosphere.

After a pause in the conversation, Auguste asked Paul, "Are you married?"

"No," Paul replied.

"Good," Auguste said eagerly. "Are you engaged?"

"No," said Paul, puzzled by Auguste's questions.

"Ah, wonderful!" Auguste exclaimed, "Would you like to go up into the stratosphere in a balloon with me? We could study the cosmic rays!"

In 1930, this was a dangerous proposal. The stratosphere begins 6 to 8 miles above Earth's surface. It is deadly cold and lacks enough oxygen for survival. Paul knew that no one had ever been up there and returned alive. Balloons had only open-air baskets. Even airplanes did not yet have pressurized cabins to hold in oxygen.

Auguste knew it was risky, too. That was why he wanted an assistant without a wife and family. Auguste's family accepted his determination to make the hazardous trip. Paul also felt the force of that determination. He listened to Auguste's plan. By the time the train arrived in Brussels, Belgium, where Auguste lived, Paul had agreed to be his assistant.

Auguste took care of every detail. The giant balloon was made of rubberized cotton. Attached to it was a pressurized cabin. It consisted of an airtight aluminum sphere with portholes as windows. It included a system that recycled oxygen so it would last longer. No lightweight crash helmets were available in those days, so Auguste created some out of upside-down sewing baskets. He added seat cushions for padding.

On the morning of May 27, 1931, Paul and Auguste prepared for take-off in Augsburg, Germany. As the balloon was being inflated, Auguste imagined all he would learn on this scientific adventure. Suddenly, a gust of wind rolled the cabin off its platform, and it crashed to the ground. It had only slight damage, so the launch continued as scheduled.

A few minutes later, however, the men heard a hissing sound. The cabin was leaking air. Auguste patched the leak with petroleum jelly and waited with his fingers crossed.

Communication with the ground crew would be impossible. Radio was only in its infancy, and satellite technology was decades in the future. Like the early explorers, the scientists sailed alone into an uncharted world.

By afternoon, the balloon had safely risen nearly 10 miles, well into the stratosphere. Auguste and Paul made some observations and measurements. Then they prepared for their descent, but something went wrong. The ropes that release the gas from the balloon had become tangled. The two men were stuck in the stratosphere.

Hours passed. The sun's heat raised the temperature inside the cabin to over 90 degrees. Sweating, the men eyed the gauges on the oxygen tanks in their silver bubble.

Auguste was certain that at nightfall the air in the balloon would cool, and they would start to descend. Yet even after the sun went down, the balloon did not. Around 6:00 A.M., Auguste wrote in his log, "We only have oxygen left for four hours."

In the meantime, people around the world waited for each day's newspaper to learn about the fate of the scientists. Readers were troubled by headlines that the balloon was out of control. In the midst of a worldwide economic depression, people craved hope and heroes.

Finally, the balloon started to float slowly down. Auguste and Paul landed the next night on top of a glacier—but where? They crawled from the cramped cabin. Unprepared for a freezing climate, they wrapped themselves in the balloon fabric to stay warm. At dawn, they picked their way down the ice slope. A rescue party soon caught up with them.

Shivering, Auguste asked a round man with a pointed wool hat, "Wh, wh, what country are we in?"

"Austria," the man answered. "We're near a village called Obergurgl."

Auguste Piccard and Paul Kipfer had spent 16 hours inside the sphere. They had ascended 51,775 feet, a height no one had reached before. Not only did they gather valuable scientific data, but they also proved that people could survive in pressurized cabins high above Earth. Their conquest of the stratosphere paved the way for future air and space travel. The publicity also established Obergurgl as a famous ski resort!

Using a Rubric

A rubric is an assessment tool for a piece of writing. Do you remember the questions you read on page 30? Those questions were used to make this rubric. You assign 1, 2, 3, or 4 points in each category of the rubric to tell how well the author completed certain writing tasks.

" Hi! My name is Lauren. Just like you, I'm learning how to write a historical episode. Did you think the article on pages 31–33 was clear and interesting? We can use this rubric to write one like that. Read the questions and the scoring information for each question. Then we'll use this rubric to evaluate the historical episode. "

Audience

How well does the writer introduce the historic event to the audience?

Organization

Does the story have a clear beginning, middle, and end? Does it stay focused on the event?

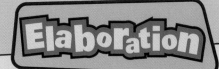

Elaboration

How well does the writer use descriptive details to create a clear picture of the historic period?

Clarification

Does the writer put the sentences in a logical order?

Conventions & Skills

Are quotations punctuated correctly?

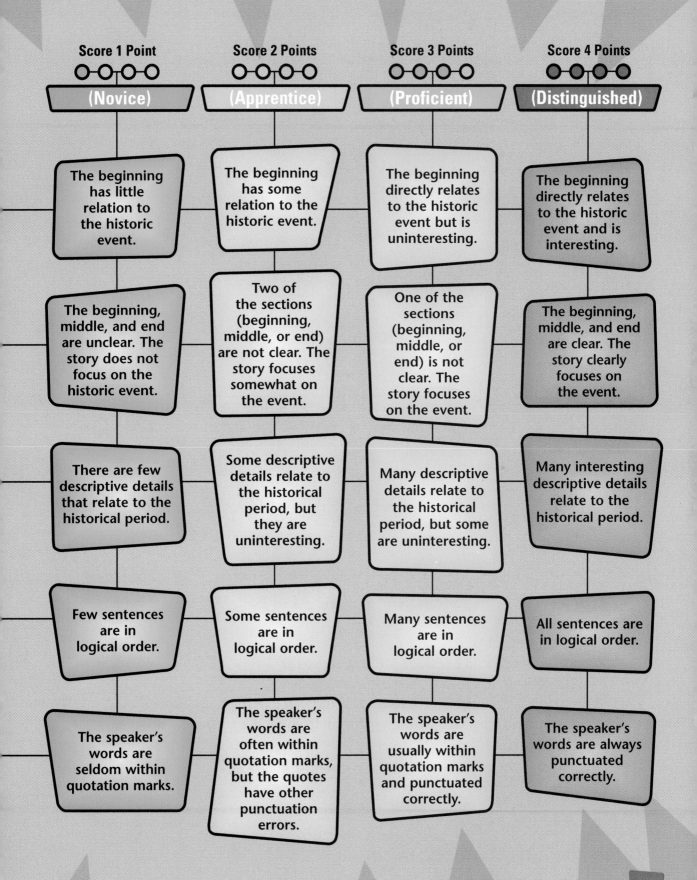

Score 1 Point
(Novice)

Score 2 Points
(Apprentice)

Score 3 Points
(Proficient)

Score 4 Points
(Distinguished)

The beginning has little relation to the historic event.

The beginning has some relation to the historic event.

The beginning directly relates to the historic event but is uninteresting.

The beginning directly relates to the historic event and is interesting.

The beginning, middle, and end are unclear. The story does not focus on the historic event.

Two of the sections (beginning, middle, or end) are not clear. The story focuses somewhat on the event.

One of the sections (beginning, middle, or end) is not clear. The story focuses on the event.

The beginning, middle, and end are clear. The story clearly focuses on the event.

There are few descriptive details that relate to the historical period.

Some descriptive details relate to the historical period, but they are uninteresting.

Many descriptive details relate to the historical period, but some are uninteresting.

Many interesting descriptive details relate to the historical period.

Few sentences are in logical order.

Some sentences are in logical order.

Many sentences are in logical order.

All sentences are in logical order.

The speaker's words are seldom within quotation marks.

The speaker's words are often within quotation marks, but the quotes have other punctuation errors.

The speaker's words are usually within quotation marks and punctuated correctly.

The speaker's words are always punctuated correctly.

Using a Rubric
to Study the Model

Discuss each question on the rubric with your classmates. Find words and sentences in the story that help you answer each one. Use the rubric to assess how well Kim Lee's historical episode did on each question.

How well does the writer introduce the historic event to the audience?

> The writer uses an interesting and puzzling conversation to introduce the historic event. The event was Auguste Piccard going up in the stratosphere in a hot-air balloon. Remember this part?

After a pause in the conversation, Auguste asked Paul, "Are you married?"

"No," Paul replied.

"Good," Auguste said eagerly. "Are you engaged?"

"No," said Paul, puzzled by Auguste's questions.

"Ah, wonderful!" Auguste exclaimed, "Would you like to go up into the stratosphere in a balloon with me? We could study the cosmic rays!"

Does the story have a clear beginning, middle, and end? Does it stay focused on the event?

" I can see a clear beginning, middle, and end, can't you? I already mentioned on page 36 how the author introduces the characters and the historic event in the beginning of the story.

"In the middle part, she explains what happens during the trip, including the problems. Here's the part where she describes a problem they had during the launch. "

On the morning of May 27, 1931, Paul and Auguste prepared for take-off in Augsburg, Germany. As the balloon was being inflated, Auguste imagined all he would learn on this scientific adventure. Suddenly, a gust of wind rolled the cabin off its platform, and it crashed to the ground.

" Toward the end, all the problems are solved. At the very end, the writer tells what happened after the balloon trip and why the trip was important. All the way through, she focuses on the historic event—the balloon trip. "

Auguste Piccard and Paul Kipfer had spent 16 hours inside the sphere. They had ascended 51,775 feet, a height no one had reached before. Not only did they gather valuable scientific data, but they also proved that people could survive in pressurized cabins high above Earth. Their conquest of the stratosphere paved the way for future air and space travel. The publicity also established Obergurgl as a famous ski resort!

How well does the writer use descriptive details to create a clear picture of the historic period?

> ❝ I found lots of examples of details that the writer included about this period. They really helped me understand what the world was like at the time of the balloon trip. ❞

Balloons had only open-air baskets. Even airplanes did not yet have pressurized cabins to hold in oxygen.

No lightweight crash helmets were available in those days, so Auguste created some out of upside-down sewing baskets. He added seat cushions for padding.

Communication with the ground crew would be impossible. Radio was only in its infancy, and satellite technology was decades in the future. Like the early explorers, the scientists sailed alone into an uncharted world.

In the meantime, people around the world waited for each day's newspaper to learn about the fate of the scientists. Readers were troubled by headlines that the balloon was out of control. In the midst of a worldwide economic depression, people craved hope and heroes.

> I think the sentences are in a logical order. The writer uses mostly chronological order—she describes the events in the order they happened. See how each sentence tells what happened next?

By afternoon, the balloon had safely risen nearly 10 miles, well into the stratosphere. Auguste and Paul made some observations and measurements. Then they prepared for their descent, but something went wrong. The ropes that release the gas from the balloon had become tangled. The two men were stuck in the stratosphere.

Hours passed. The sun's heat raised the temperature inside the cabin to over 90 degrees. Sweating, the men eyed the gauges on the oxygen tanks in their silver bubble.

Auguste was certain that at nightfall the air in the balloon would cool, and they would start to descend. Yet even after the sun went down, the balloon did not. Around 6:00 A.M., Auguste wrote in his log, "We only have oxygen left for four hours."

"This writer sure knows how to use quotes. Every time a character speaks in this story, his exact words have quotation marks around them. The rest of the punctuation for each quotation is correct, too. Check it out!"

Shivering, Auguste asked a round man with a pointed wool hat, "Wh, wh, what country are we in?"

"Austria," the man answered. "We're near a village called Obergurgl."

"Now it's my turn to write!

Now I'm going to use the rubric to help me write a historical episode. Read along and see how well I do."

LAUREN

Writer of a Historical Episode

Name:	Lauren
Home:	New York
Hobbies:	hiking and fossil hunting
Favorite Fossil:	clam from 300 million years ago, found near the shore of Cayuga Lake
Assignment:	historical episode

Prewriting

Gather

Choose a historical event. Take notes on that event from several reliable sources.

" I like to hike and dig for fossils. I live close to Cardiff, New York, which is where the Cardiff Giant was buried. (It wasn't really a giant!) When my teacher asked us to write a historical episode, I decided to write about the giant.

"To prepare, I read an overview of the event in an encyclopedia. Then I looked at a library book and some reliable Web sites on the topic. Here are some of the notes I took. "

My Notes on the Cardiff Giant

* 1866: George Hull heard some people talk about giants on Earth – he got an idea

* 1868: Hull sent a huge chunk of gypsum from Ft. Dodge to Chicago

* stonecutters made 10-foot man, twisted body, calm face – acid to make it look old

* Hull buried statue near Cardiff, NY, on farm of William Newell, his relative who was in on hoax

* Oct. 16, 1869: well diggers found giant, Newell put up tent, charged 300–500 people daily to see statue

* people say they saw Hull and wagon with box the year before – Hull admits hoax on Dec. 10

* "There's a sucker born every minute." – Hull's partner

* giant stored, exhibited at fairs, bought by Farmers' Museum in Cooperstown, NY, in 1947

* period: after Civil War, mid-Victorian Age – growth in business, science, and technology (no cars or phone)

Go to page 18 in the **Practice** the Strategy **Notebook!**

Prewriting

Organize

Organize my notes into a story map.

"The **Rubric** stresses organization. I'm going to use a story map to organize the information in my notes. The story map will help me think about the information I've gathered and find a way to present this episode so the audience can easily follow along."

Story Map

A **story map** organizes the setting, characters, problem, plot, and ending of a story.

Setting – Time: 1866–1869
Setting – Main place: farm near Cardiff, NY

Main characters: George Hull, William Newell, well diggers, scientist

Problem: Hull has to convince people that a stone sculpture is a giant fossilized prehistoric man and get them to pay to see it.

Plot/Events: Hull learns about the giant story, comes up with a hoax, has a stone sculpture made, has it buried on a relative's farm, it's discovered, people pay to see it, Hull sells part ownership of it. People start to doubt Hull's claims and check into them.

Ending/Resolution: Hull admits the hoax. The giant is moved around for years. It finally ends up in a NY museum.

Go to page 20 in the **Practice the Strategy Notebook!**

Drafting

Write

Draft my episode. Include a clear beginning, middle, and end. Keep the focus on the event.

"Now that I'm ready to write, I need to think about my audience. The historical episodes that my class is writing are going to be part of a display at the town library, so the community is my audience.

"I need a clear beginning, middle, and end for my episode. I also need to focus on the historic event the whole time. I think I'll present the plot in the order it happened. That will help me keep the story clear and focused on the event. To grab the audience at the beginning, I'll hint at what's to come. This is my first draft, so I'll just write now and worry about spelling and grammar later."

clear beginning that introduces the historic event

The Cardiff Giant

[1st DRAFT]

In 1866 George Hull ~~from~~ of Binghamton, New York visited his sister in Iowa. ~~On~~ During his visit, he learned that some people believed there were giants on Earth long ago. That gave Hull an idea. Hull began to make plans to put his own giant on Earth.

Two years later, Hull returned to Iowa. He sent a block of gypsum ~~to~~ from a quarry near Fort Dodge to Chicago. Then he hired stone-cutters to carve it into a man. Hull wanted it to look like a prehistoric man, so he "aged" it with acid. To create the look of skin pores, he poked the stone with darning needles.

When it was all done, Hull took it to the farm of William Newell, a relative who was in on the idea. Newell lived near Cardiff, New York, south of Syracuse Together they buried the stone giant behind the barn. Then they waited.

A year later on October 16, 1869 Newell hired two men to dig a well there. A few feet down, they hit something. I declare, someone has been buried here! said one of the workmen.

clear middle that stays focused on the historic event

At first, many thought the sculpture really was a petrified man from an earler time. the region was known for it's fossils.

As word spread, hundreds of people came each day to see the strange thing. The Cardiff Giant was an instant celebrity. Newell charged 25 cents admission. He kept raising the price.

Most scientists thought it was a trick. Maybe it was an ~~old~~ anceint statue carved by native Americans or early white settlers.

Hull ~~was~~ thought his hoax would soon be known, so he sold part the sculpture to some business people and then the giant was moved to Syracuse and other cities. An investigation started. People said Hull was traveling with a big box the year before. Hull admitted the hoax. Hull's partner said "there's a sucker born every minute"

The Cardiff Giant toured for a while, but then went into storage. Then it was shown at fairs in Iowa and New York. At one time it was in ~~a~~ somebody's play room. In 1947, the Farmers' Museum in Cooperstown, New York, bought the giant.

Today visitors to the museum stand under a tent just like the first visitors did to see the Cardiff Giant, America's greatest hoax.

clear end, still focusing on the historic event

Go to page 21 in the Practice the Strategy Notebook!

Revising

Elaborate

Add details that create a clear picture of the historical period.

❝ Now it's time to start revising. The **Rubric** says that including descriptive details will help my audience understand the historical period.

"My historical episode occurred between 1866 and 1869. That was right after the end of the Civil War, when there were no cars or telephones. I took notes on this period, and I need to include details in my story that bring it to life. I'll start with the first paragraph. How's this? ❞

Historical Period

A **historical period** is a setting for an event, usually in the past. Colonial America, the 1960s, and the Victorian Age are all historical periods.

[2nd DRAFT]

descriptive detail →

It was ⊙

~~In~~ 1866 The Civil War had just ended, and the nation was looking toward a brighter future. George Hull of Binghamton, New York visited [was] [ing]
his sister in Iowa. During his visit, he learned that some people believed
there were giants on Earth long ago. That gave Hull an idea. On the long [for a new business venture]
trip home by steamboat and train, Hull began to ~~make~~ plans to put his [hatch a]
own giant on Earth.

← descriptive detail

Go to page 24 in the **Practice the Strategy Notebook!**

Revising

Clarify
Put the sentences in logical order so the story is easy to follow.

" The **Rubric** stresses that the sentences in the story should be in logical order. I read my second draft to my friend Casey, and he helped me realize that a few sentences were out of order.

READ TO A PARTNER

"I rearranged the sentences in the two paragraphs below to make them clearer. In the first paragraph, the sentence that told what the paragraph was about was buried in the middle. I put it first.

"In the second paragraph, I moved another sentence. It explained why scientists thought the giant was a fake, so I put it after the first sentence. Aren't both paragraphs easier to understand now? "

[3rd DRAFT]

moved sentence

The Cardiff Giant was an instant celebrity. As word spread,
~~gaze at~~
hundreds of people came each day to ~~see~~ the strange marvel. Four
stagecoaches a day ran between the Syracuse train station and
Cardiff. (The Cardiff Giant was an instant celebrity.) Newell put a tent
over the site and charged 25 cents admission. As the visitors
increased, so did the fee.

moved sentence

fake.
Most scientists were certain it was a ~~trick~~ Geology was a new
science in the mid-1800s, but paleontologists knew that flesh could
not be turned to stone. This judgment led to another theory: Maybe
gypsum   ancient
the giant was an ~~anceint~~ statue carved by native Americans or early
white settlers. (Geology was a new science in the mid-1800s, but
paleontologists knew that flesh could not be turned to stone.)

the Strategy
Go to page 25 in the **Practice Notebook!**

Narrative Writing • Historical Episode

Editing

Proofread

Check to see that quotations are punctuated correctly.

> Now I need to check my draft for errors. I will check my spelling, capitalization, and punctuation.
>
> "Then I'll check my quotes extra carefully. If they aren't punctuated correctly, the reader will be confused about what the speakers said.
>
> "Part of my story is on the next page, so you can see the kinds of errors I corrected."

Quotations

A **quotation** is the exact words of a speaker or a writer. Use quotation marks at the beginning and end of a quotation. Use a comma to separate the speaker's words from the rest of the sentence. If a quotation is a complete sentence, begin it with a capital letter. Add the correct end punctuation before the last quotation mark.

Examples: Hull said, "You must tell no one that you carved the giant."

"My lips are sealed," the stonecutter said.

"I'm going to be rich!" Hull exclaimed.

Extra Practice

See **Quotations** (pages CS 4–CS 5) in the back of this book.

Proofreading Marks

⌐ Indent.

≡ Make a capital.

/ Make a small letter.

∧ Add something.

ℒ Take out something.

⊙ Add a period.

⌗ New paragraph

ⓈⓅ Spelling error

[4th DRAFT]

When the sculpture was completed, Hull shipped it to the farm of William Newell, a relative who was in on the ~~skeem~~. ⓈⓅ scheme Newell lived near Cardiff, New York, south of Syracuse⊙ Together they buried the giant behind Newell's barn. Wiping the dirt from his hands, Hull said∧"We'll make a fortune off the fools, but we must wait until the time is right."

A year later∧a large bed of fossils was discovered nearby. Hull sent a mysterⓈⓅyous telegram to Newell. It ~~said~~∧read, "Strike while the iron is hot⊙"

⌗ On October 16, 1869∧Newell hired two men to dig a well at a certain spot near the barn. A few feet down, their shovels clanked against something. "I declare, someone has been buried here!" said one of the workmen as he uncovered a stone foot.

⌗ He cleared away the rest of the dirt and ran to fetch Newell. Newell peered down into the pit and ruⓈⓅbed his beard. A silent stone giant stared back. ~~It's~~ Its body was twisted as if in pain,∧but its face had a peaceful expression. Newell said,∧"ride into town, boys, and tell them what we've got here."

quotes punctuated correctly

quote punctuated correctly

quote punctuated correctly

Go to page 26 in the **Practice** the Strategy ∧**Notebook!**

Narrative Writing • Historical Episode

49

Publishing

Share Include my historical episode in a library display.

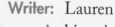

Writer:	Lauren
Assignment:	historical episode
Topic:	the Cardiff Giant hoax
Audience:	people in the community
Method of Publication:	library display
Reason for Choice:	The town library is setting up displays on historical periods.

" Our town library is putting together displays on historical periods. The librarians asked our class to help. My historical episode will be part of the display for the nineteenth century. This is how I published my story. "

1. I checked my story one more time for mistakes.
2. Then I printed a clean copy of my story.
3. At the top I put my title and added "by Lauren."
4. I added a historical advertisement for the Cardiff Giant. I might make a model of the giant later.
5. I helped the librarians arrange the display.

The Cardiff Giant

by Lauren

It was 1866. The Civil War had just ended, and the nation was looking toward a brighter future. George Hull of Binghamton, New York, was visiting his sister in Iowa. During his visit, he learned that some people believed there were giants on Earth long ago. That gave Hull an idea for a new business venture. On the long trip home by steamboat and train, Hull began to hatch a plan to put a giant on Earth.

Two years later, Hull returned to Iowa. He shipped a 3,000-pound block of gypsum from a quarry near Fort Dodge to Chicago. Then he hired stonecutters to secretly carve the hunk of rock into the shape of a man more than 10 feet tall.

Hull wanted the statue to look like a petrified prehistoric man, so he "aged" it with acid. To create the appearance of skin pores, he pounded the stone with darning needles.

When the sculpture was completed, Hull shipped it to the farm of William Newell, a relative who was in on the scheme. Newell lived near Cardiff, New York, south of Syracuse. Together they buried the giant behind Newell's barn. Wiping the dirt from his hands, Hull said, "We'll make a fortune off the fools, but we must wait until the time is right."

A year later, a large bed of fossils was discovered nearby. Hull sent a mysterious telegram to Newell. It read, "Strike while the iron is hot."

On October 16, 1869, Newell hired two men to dig a well at a certain spot near the barn. A few feet down, their shovels clanked against something. "I declare, someone has been buried here!" said one of the workmen as he uncovered a stone foot.

He cleared away the rest of the dirt and ran to fetch Newell. Newell peered down into the pit and rubbed his beard. A silent stone giant stared back. Its body was twisted as if in pain, but its face had a peaceful expression. Newell said, "Ride into town, boys, and tell them what we've got here."

The Cardiff Giant was an instant celebrity. As word spread, hundreds of people came each day to gaze at the strange marvel. Four stagecoaches a day ran between the Syracuse train station and Cardiff. Newell put a tent over the site and charged 25 cents admission. As the number of visitors increased, so did the fee.

At first, many thought the sculpture really was a petrified man from an earlier time. After all, the region was known for its fossils. Recent advances in science and technology made the public believe that almost anything was possible.

Most scientists were certain it was a fake. Geology was a new science in the mid-1800s, but paleontologists knew that flesh could not be turned to stone. This judgment led to another theory: Maybe the gypsum giant was an ancient statue carved by Native Americans or early white settlers.

Hull suspected his hoax would soon be revealed. He sold part ownership of the giant to a group of local business people. It was moved to Syracuse and then toured other cities in New York.

In the meantime, an investigation was started. Local people remembered they had seen Hull traveling with a large wooden crate on a wagon the year before. On December 10, Hull admitted the hoax. One of Hull's partners commented, "There's a sucker born every minute."

The Cardiff Giant toured for a while and then went into storage. Later it appeared at fairs in Iowa and New York. It was even stored in a child's playroom for a while. In 1947, the Farmers' Museum in Cooperstown, New York, bought the giant.

Today, visitors to the museum stand under a tent just like the first visitors did in 1869. There, they ponder the Cardiff Giant, America's greatest hoax.

USING the Rubric for Assessment

Go to pages 28–29 in the **Practice** the Strategy **Notebook!** Use that rubric to assess Lauren's paper. Try using the rubric to assess your own writing.

your own NARRATIVE writing

Social Studies

Put the strategies you practiced in this unit to work to write your own eyewitness account, historical episode, or both! You can:

- develop the Your Own Writing pages of the *Practice the Strategy Notebook*;

- pick an idea below and write something new;

- choose another idea of your own.

Be sure to follow the steps in the writing process. Use the rubrics in this unit to assess your writing.

Eyewitness Account	Historical Episode
• a parade • an ethnic festival • a holiday celebration • a historical reenactment	• the discovery of King Tut's tomb • the first successful airplane flight • the first telephone call • the fall of the Berlin Wall

portfolio

School–Home Connection

Keep a writing portfolio. Think about adding the activities from the *Practice the Strategy Notebook* to your writing portfolio. You may want to take your portfolio home to share.

EXPOSITORY
writing
explains something to the reader.

1

Business Letter

2

Summary

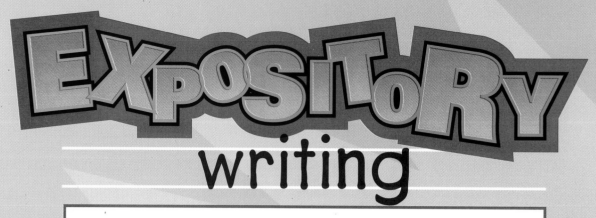

writing

Business Letter

In this chapter, you will work with one kind of expository writing: a **business letter**.

A **business letter** is written for a specific purpose, such as to inform, persuade, ask for information, compliment, or criticize. This kind of letter has six main parts: the heading, inside address, salutation (greeting), body, closing, and signature.

Read the questions below. Then read the letter, keeping the questions in mind.

 Does the letter have a businesslike tone?

 Are the points in the letter organized in order of importance?

 Does the writer include all the necessary information?

 Is the purpose for writing stated in the first paragraph and restated in the concluding paragraph?

 Are all six parts of a business letter included? Are homophones used correctly?

heading

Tiny Tikes Daycare Center
333 Willow Park Road
Lexington, KY 40509
May 4, 2002

Customer Service Manager
Real Cereal, Inc.
2128 N. Jarvis St.
Trenton, NJ 08620

inside address

Dear Customer Service Manager: ← **salutation**

body

   I own a daycare center that serves breakfast cereal to children in the morning. I am usually pleased with Real Cereal products. However, the "new and improved" Oaty Boats is not satisfactory. I refuse to continue to buy Oaty Boats until Real Cereal addresses its problems.

   The boats now taste like cardboard, and they sink instead of floating. Furthermore, the food dye in the new boats turns the milk in the bowl greenish brown.

   In addition, I do not like a recent commercial that shows Oaty Boats as destroyers in a battle. What does your ad tell children about the uses of a boat? It tells them only that a boat is used to fight.

   There are sailboats, tugboats, and freighters in Oaty Boats, too. It would be more positive and educational to show children a range of boats and a range of uses. You're as responsible for molding their young minds as I am. I would like to see more thoughtful advertising from Real Cereal. Remember, it takes a community to raise a child.

   Please change the cereal back to its original flavor and natural color. Also, think more carefully about how you use boats in your advertising. Until Oaty Boats is returned to its original form, I will no longer purchase it for the children in my daycare center.

closing ⟶ Sincerely,

signature ⟶ *Jean Silverstone*

Jean Silverstone, Director

Using a Rubric

A rubric is a tool that lists "what counts" for a piece of writing. You assign 1, 2, 3, or 4 points to tell how well the author handled certain writing tasks.

Remember the questions you read on page 56? Those questions were used to make this rubric.

" Hi! My name is Jesse. I'm learning how to write a business letter like the one on page 57. I'm going to use this rubric to help me. You can, too. First, read the questions. Next, read the scoring information for each question. Then we'll use this rubric to evaluate the business letter. "

Audience

Does the letter have a businesslike tone?

Organization

Are the points in the letter organized in order of importance?

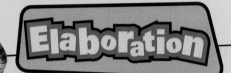

Elaboration

Does the writer include all the necessary information?

Clarification

Is the purpose for writing stated in the first paragraph and restated in the concluding paragraph?

Conventions & Skills

Are all six parts of a business letter included? Are homophones used correctly?

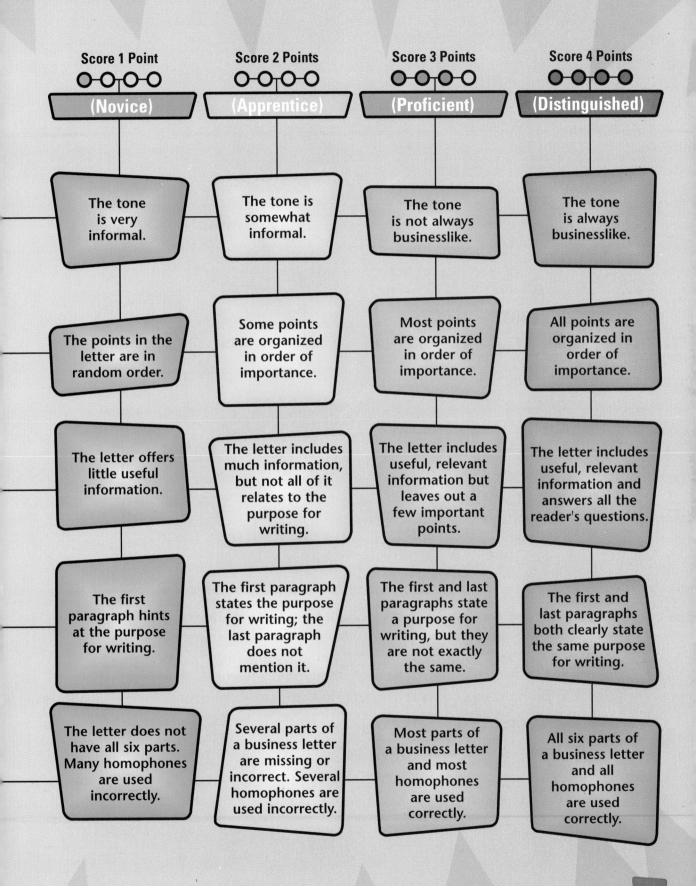

Score 1 Point (Novice)	Score 2 Points (Apprentice)	Score 3 Points (Proficient)	Score 4 Points (Distinguished)
The tone is very informal.	The tone is somewhat informal.	The tone is not always businesslike.	The tone is always businesslike.
The points in the letter are in random order.	Some points are organized in order of importance.	Most points are organized in order of importance.	All points are organized in order of importance.
The letter offers little useful information.	The letter includes much information, but not all of it relates to the purpose for writing.	The letter includes useful, relevant information but leaves out a few important points.	The letter includes useful, relevant information and answers all the reader's questions.
The first paragraph hints at the purpose for writing.	The first paragraph states the purpose for writing; the last paragraph does not mention it.	The first and last paragraphs state a purpose for writing, but they are not exactly the same.	The first and last paragraphs both clearly state the same purpose for writing.
The letter does not have all six parts. Many homophones are used incorrectly.	Several parts of a business letter are missing or incorrect. Several homophones are used incorrectly.	Most parts of a business letter and most homophones are used correctly.	All six parts of a business letter and all homophones are used correctly.

Using a Rubric
to Study the Model

Discuss each question on the rubric with your classmates. Find words and sentences in Jean Silverstone's letter that help you answer each one.

Does the letter have a businesslike tone?

"Yes. This writer uses a businesslike tone throughout her letter. For example, she is angry about the commercial, but she doesn't use angry words. She might have said something like this: 'There are other kinds of boats in your cereal! Why didn't you show them in your commercial? You are being totally irresponsible!'

"Instead, she uses a tone that is polite and formal. Read how she does it."

There are sailboats, tugboats, and freighters in Oaty Boats, too. It would be more positive and educational to show children a range of boats and a range of uses. You're as responsible for molding their young minds as I am. I would like to see more thoughtful advertising from Real Cereal. Remember, it takes a community to raise a child.

Are the points in the letter organized in order of importance?

"Yes, I think so. You just read her first paragraph where she explains her most important point: that she isn't going to buy Oaty Boats anymore. In the next paragraph, she explains problems with the cereal's taste and appearance.

"Then the writer criticizes the Oaty Boats commercial. She probably mentions this point last because it isn't as important to her as problems with how the cereal tastes and looks."

The boats now taste like cardboard, and they sink instead of floating. Furthermore, the food dye in the new boats turns the milk in the bowl greenish brown.

In addition, I do not like a recent commercial that shows Oaty Boats as destroyers in a battle. What does your ad tell children about the uses of a boat? It tells them only that a boat is used to fight.

Elaboration

Does the writer include all the necessary information?

"I can't think of any other information that she could have included. She explains that she used to buy Oaty Boats. In the paragraphs above, she tells why she stopped buying them. At the end of the letter, she says what she would like the cereal company to do.

"The letter even includes her name and address, in case the cereal company wants to contact her. She didn't leave out any important information that I can see."

Clarification

Is the purpose for writing stated in the first paragraph and restated in the concluding paragraph?

" My teacher told us that business people want to know right away why you're writing. This writer starts her letter by stating her purpose: to tell Real Cereal that she won't buy the new Oaty Boats until the company fixes the problems with it. "

I own a daycare center that serves breakfast cereal to children in the morning. I am usually pleased with Real Cereal products. However, the "new and improved" Oaty Boats is not satisfactory. I refuse to continue to buy Oaty Boats until Real Cereal addresses its problems.

" Then the writer repeats her purpose for writing in her last paragraph. "

Please change the cereal back to its original flavor and natural color. Also, think more carefully about how you use boats in your advertising. Until Oaty Boats is returned to its original form, I will no longer purchase it for the children in my daycare center.

Conventions & Skills

Are all six parts of a business letter included? Are homophones used correctly?

" The writer set up all six parts of a business letter perfectly. She also used homophones correctly. When she had to choose among words such as **to/too/two** and **your/you're**, she chose the right word every time. "

" **Now it's my turn to write!**

To see how I apply good writing strategies in a business letter, stick around! I'll use what I learned from the model and the rubric. "

Jesse

Writer of a Business Letter

EXIT 82B
40 WEST
Memphis

Name: Jesse
Home: Tennessee
Hobbies: playing blues guitar, writing blues songs
Favorite Blues Song: "Crossroad Blues" by Robert Johnson
Assignment: business letter

63

Prewriting

Gather
Pick something to praise or criticize.
List reasons for my praise or criticism.

"I live in Tennessee. It's known for country music, but I'm into the blues. One of our local radio stations, KTNT, started a blues show a few months ago. It's called 'Down to the Blues.'

"When my teacher said we were going to write a business letter, I decided to write to KTNT to praise that program. To prepare, I used my braille note-taker to make a list of reasons why I like the new blues program. This is my list."

Reasons Why I Like "Down to the Blues"

- The program plays songs by classic blues artists like Robert Johnson, Blind Lemon Jefferson, and Ma Rainey.

- It also plays songs by modern blues artists like B. B. King, Luther Allison, and Koko Taylor.

- I'm learning a lot about the blues from the show. One night a week, it has a guest musician. I learn all about the guest artists and their music. Once a month, a blues guitarist teaches listeners a new blues song! No other station does that.

- My dog, Muddy, loves to howl the blues! He's named after Muddy Waters.

- The show is on from 7 to 9 P.M. on two weeknights, so I can listen to it after I finish my homework.

Go to page 30 in the **Practice** the Strategy **Notebook!**

Prewriting

Organize
Organize my reasons from most important to least important.

" According to the **Rubric**, I should organize the reasons in my letter by order of importance. I'll start with the most important and end with the least important.

"I'll use an order-of-importance organizer. The upside-down triangle shows that my points go from most to least important. "

Order-of-Importance Organizer

An **order-of-importance organizer** shows the main points in order of importance. The points can be ordered from most to least important or from least to most important.

I learn a lot about the blues from the show.

The program plays songs by classic and modern blues artists.

most important reason

The show is on at a good time— after I have done my homework.

My dog likes to howl to the blues.

least important reason

Go to page 32 in the **Practice** the Strategy **Notebook!**

Drafting

Write

Draft my letter. State my purpose for writing in the first paragraph.

" Now I'm ready to write. The first category on the **Rubric** is audience. The KTNT station manager will be my audience.

"In a business letter, I know I need to make my purpose for writing clear to my audience in the first paragraph. My purpose is to praise KTNT for its new blues show. You can read my first paragraph and the rest of my first draft on the next page. Do you think my first paragraph makes my purpose clear?

"As you can see, I used my first draft to write down all the ideas I wanted in my letter. I'll do my best with spelling and grammar and correct any mistakes in later drafts. That's when I'll add the other parts of a business letter, too. "

Purpose for Writing

The **purpose for writing** is the reason for writing, the writer's goal. The purpose might be to inform, persuade, ask for information, compliment, or criticize.

Dear station manager,

Luther Allison said "If you don't like the blues, you've got a hole in your soul." He's a blues musician. I love the blues! I'm writing to tell you how much I love you're new blues show. Their is sooo much to learn.

purpose for writing Your the only station around whose Blues program ~~has~~ teaches songs on the air. Its an entertaining way to learn stuff. I also learn about different blues musicians There an inspiration.

I really like it how the show plays songs by classic blues artists. It plays songs by modern blues artists to. I play blues guitar. Their music influences my songs. My parents leave me lissen too the show ~~when~~ after I do my homework.

~~Muddy~~ My dog Muddy also likes your cool program. Muddy houls the blues. He's not as good as Muddy waters (whose his favorite blues singer).

Go to page 34 in the **Practice** the Strategy **Notebook!**

Revising

Elaborate
Make sure I include all the necessary information.

❝The **Rubric** reminds me to include all the necessary information. When I listened to my letter, I realized that I hadn't been clear about which show I liked. I needed to add more information, like the name of the show and when it's on. Here are the changes I made. Now they'll know which show I mean!❞

[2nd DRAFT]

Luther Allison said "If you don't like the blues, you've got a hole in your soul." He's a blues musician. I love the blues! I'm writing to tell you how much I love you're new ~~blues~~ show "Down to the Blues." Their is sooo much to learn.

added information

I really like it how the show plays songs by classic blues artists. It plays songs by modern blues artists to. I play blues guitar. Their music influences my songs. My parents leave me lissen to the show after I do my homework.

I hope that KTNT will continue to broadcast it's blues program to nights a week at 7 P.M.

added information

Go to page 35 in the **Practice** the Strategy **Notebook!**

Revising

Clarify

Remember to restate my purpose for writing in my last paragraph. Check to see that I have used a businesslike tone.

> After I wrote my second draft on my braille note-taker, I read it to my partner, Tyler, and I listened to it. He liked it, but he reminded me that the **Rubric** says a business letter should restate the purpose for writing in the last paragraph.
>
> "So I left the part about Muddy, but I also told the station manager again that I like the show."

READ TO A PARTNER

[3rd DRAFT]

restates the purpose for writing

My dog Muddy ~~also likes your~~ cool program. Muddy howls the
    and I   want to thank you for this

blues. He's not as good as Muddy waters (whose his favorite blues
    He's learning the blues from your show, just like I am.
singer).

> Tyler also mentioned that some of the words I used sounded like kids talking to their friends. I need to use a more serious tone. You can see how I improved this paragraph.

businesslike tone   area
Your the only station ~~around~~ whose Blues program teaches songs
            add to my understanding of blues   discover more
on the air. Its an entertaining way to ~~learn stuff.~~ I also ~~learn~~ about
    various
~~different~~ blues musicians. There an inspiration.

Go to page 36 in the **Practice** the Strategy **Notebook!**

Editing

Proofread

Check to see that all six parts of a business letter are included. Make sure homophones are used correctly.

> It's time to check my draft for errors. I'll work with my partner, Tyler.

Homophones

Homophones are words that sound alike but have different spellings and meanings. They include *its/it's, there/their/they're, two/to/too, your/you're,* and *whose/who's.* Make sure you use these words correctly.

Extra Practice
See **Homophones** (pages CS 6–CS 7) in the back of this book.

The Six Parts of a Business Letter

• Place the **heading** about an inch from the top of the page. Include the sender's complete address, followed by the date.

• Place the **inside address** below the heading. Include the reader's complete address. Place the reader's title below his or her name.

• Place the **salutation** (greeting) below the inside address. Add a colon after the salutation.

• Place the **body** of the letter below the salutation.

• Place the **closing** below the body. Use a formal closing such as *Yours truly* or *Sincerely.* Add a comma after the closing.

• Type your full name below the closing. Leave enough space for your **signature** between the closing and your typed name.

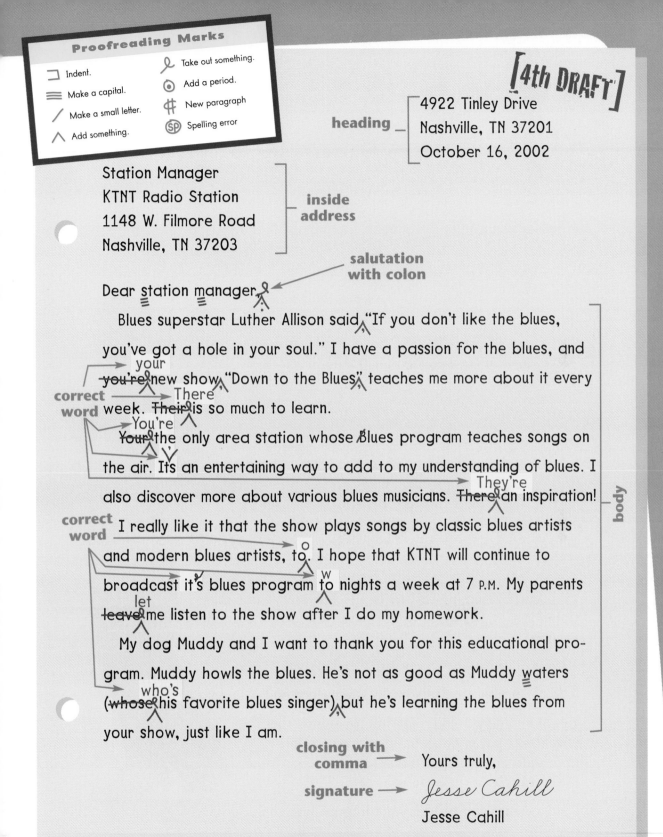

Proofreading Marks

⊐ Indent.
≡ Make a capital.
∕ Make a small letter.
∧ Add something.
ℰ Take out something.
⊙ Add a period.
New paragraph.
SP Spelling error

[4th DRAFT]

heading — 4922 Tinley Drive
Nashville, TN 37201
October 16, 2002

Station Manager
KTNT Radio Station   inside
1148 W. Filmore Road   address
Nashville, TN 37203

salutation with colon

Dear station manager,

Blues superstar Luther Allison said, "If you don't like the blues, you've got a hole in your soul." I have a passion for the blues, and

your
correct — you're new show, "Down to the Blues," teaches me more about it every
word   There
week. Their is so much to learn.

You're
Your the only area station whose Blues program teaches songs on the air. Its an entertaining way to add to my understanding of blues. I also discover more about various blues musicians. There an inspiration!
They're

correct
word   I really like it that the show plays songs by classic blues artists
o
and modern blues artists, to. I hope that KTNT will continue to
w
broadcast it's blues program to nights a week at 7 P.M. My parents
let
leave me listen to the show after I do my homework.

My dog Muddy and I want to thank you for this educational pro-gram. Muddy howls the blues. He's not as good as Muddy waters
who's
(whose his favorite blues singer) but he's learning the blues from your show, just like I am.

closing with comma → Yours truly,

signature → *Jesse Cahill*
Jesse Cahill

body

the Strategy
Go to page 38 in the **Practice Notebook!**

Expository Writing • Business Letter

Publishing

Share Mail my business letter to my reader.

Writer:	Jesse
Assignment:	business letter
Topic:	a new blues radio program
Audience:	radio station manager
Method of Publication:	mail letter
Reason for Choice:	Mailing is the best way to send my letter to my reader.

" After we edited and proofread our business letters, our teacher asked us to mail them to our readers. This is how I published my letter. "

1. To begin, I asked my partner to check my letter one more time for mistakes that I might have missed in my braille version.

2. I made a clean copy of my letter and signed it.

3. Then I put my letter in a business envelope and sealed it.

4. I used my mom's old typewriter to address the envelope. I put my name and address in the upper-left corner. I put the reader's address in the lower middle of the envelope.

5. I put a stamp on my letter and dropped it in the mailbox.

4922 Tinley Drive
Nashville, TN 37201
October 16, 20__

Station Manager
KTNT Radio Station
1148 W. Filmore Road
Nashville, TN 37203

Dear Station Manager:

Blues superstar Luther Allison said, "If you don't like the blues, you've got a hole in your soul." I have a passion for the blues, and your new show, "Down to the Blues," teaches me more about it every week. There is so much to learn.

You're the only area station whose blues program teaches songs on the air. It's an entertaining way to add to my understanding of blues. I also discover more about various blues musicians. They're an inspiration!

I really like it that the show plays songs by classic blues artists and modern blues artists, too. I hope that KTNT will continue to broadcast its blues program two nights a week at 7 P.M. My parents let me listen to the show after I do my homework.

My dog Muddy and I want to thank you for this educational program. Muddy howls the blues. He's not as good as Muddy Waters (who's his favorite blues singer), but he's learning the blues from your show, just like I am.

Yours truly,

Jesse Cahill

Jesse Cahill

USING the Rubric for Assessment

Go to pages 40–41 in the **Practice** the Strategy **Notebook!** Use that rubric to assess Jesse's paper. Try using the rubric to assess your own writing.

EXPOSITORY writing

Summary

In this chapter, you will work with one kind of expository writing: a **summary**.

A **summary** is a short piece of writing that explains the main points of a longer selection. Your goal will be to explain the main ideas in another piece of writing, using as few words as possible.

On the next page is a summary of the magazine article on pages 76–77. Read the questions below. Then read the summary and the article. Keep these questions in mind as you read the summary.

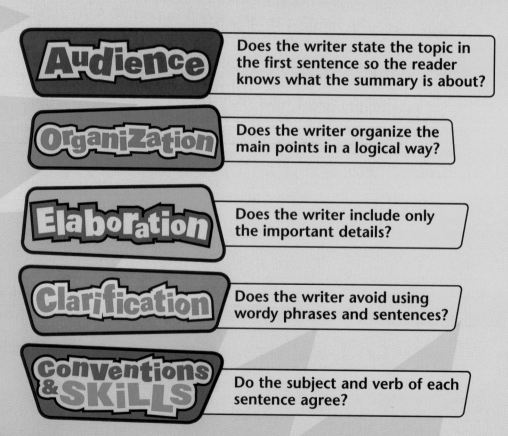

Audience Does the writer state the topic in the first sentence so the reader knows what the summary is about?

Organization Does the writer organize the main points in a logical way?

Elaboration Does the writer include only the important details?

Clarification Does the writer avoid using wordy phrases and sentences?

Conventions & Skills Do the subject and verb of each sentence agree?

"A Touch of Genius"

by Patricia Millman
Summary by Keesha Kane

Michael Naranjo is a Native American sculptor in Santa Fe, New Mexico. He chose his career when he was a boy helping his mother make pottery in the pueblo. At age 23, however, Naranjo was wounded in the Vietnam War. He was blinded and left without the complete use of one hand.

Naranjo was unsure if he would still be able to sculpt. While recovering in the hospital, he molded several clay sculptures of animals. One was so good that it was photographed for the newspaper. That convinced him to pursue his dream.

Although he cannot see, he can remember images from his past. His mind carries the images to his fingertips.

Naranjo has won awards for his work and leads sculpture workshops. His sculptures are displayed in museums and public buildings around the world. Private collectors also seek his art.

Michael A. Naranjo ▲

A Touch of Genius

by Patricia Millman

Michael Naranjo is a Native American, a Vietnam War veteran, and "a sculptor who happens to be blind." Behind this statement lies a remarkable story.

Michael grew up in the Tewa Indian pueblo of Santa Clara, New Mexico. As a boy, he roamed the scenic foothills west of the pueblo community and explored the Rio Grande, a river to the south and east. His world was enriched by the beautiful sights and sounds of the desert country.

This artist sees with his hands.

Michael's love of sculpting was born at the pueblo, too. "My mother was a potter, and I would help her fix clay," he recalls. "She gathered her clay in a place in the hills that only she knew about. Every potter has their own source of clay, and when they find that clay, they're very secretive about it.

"My mother would bring in the clay and screen it to get out anything that didn't belong, and then she would soak it in tubs. After that, she'd put the clay into a square of canvas cloth, and she'd sprinkle a different white kind of clay on top. Then she would fold this square of canvas and press on it this way and that way, and when she unfolded the canvas I could see this little log of clay inside.

"Then I would take off my shoes and perform a little dance with the clay. I would sidestep on this log of clay. I could feel the moist clay on the side of my foot and between my toes. And when I reached the other end, I'd step off the square of canvas, and she'd fold it and push it this way and that way and refold it, and I would have this little log of clay again. And once again I would perform my little dance."

Michael's dance served a very important purpose. He was blending the white clay and the brown clay to make it stronger. With this strong clay, his mother could make pots that would last a long time.

"That's probably how I started sculpting. . . playing with clay," Michael says. "Not long after that, I wanted to make figures of animals. And as they became more detailed, they became sculptures. So even way back then, I knew that what I wanted to do was be an artist someday."

▲ *One More* by Michael A. Naranjo

Seeing with His Hands

Michael's goal would not be reached easily. While serving with the Army in Vietnam, Michael was badly wounded in battle. He lost his sight and partial use of one hand. For the first time, Michael wondered if he could ever be a sculptor.

One day, while recovering in the hospital, Michael asked if he could have a small piece of clay. From it he made an inchworm.

The next sculpture Michael made, an Indian on a horse, was so good it was photographed by the newspapers. Lucky thing! Because when Michael decided to make his next sculpture, he found that the hospital didn't have any more clay. So he reshaped the Indian on a horse into a bear with a fish in its mouth.

Today, Michael has lots of material to use to make his memories come to life. "I was able to see until I was twenty-three years old, so I have a very good idea of what most things look like," he said. "So I sit, and I think about it, and I get a picture in my mind. If you close your eyes and think of . . . well, if you have a cat or a dog, you can picture this pet. The same process happens with me.

▲ Michael enjoys teaching sculpting workshops. "One step at a time and you can do it," he reminds his students.

"Once you have the material in your hand that you can mold and shape, then you can carry it over from your mind to your fingertips; and your mind tells your fingers, 'Make that bigger or smaller...' until this whole process slowly starts happening.

"Nowadays, when I make animals, I sit there and think about the days when I'd take a moment sitting on a cliff side and look down and see a deer down there or watch some turkeys walk through the forest. Or the time I followed a mountain stream and a deer stopped in this pool of water and looked at me with his huge brown eyes. It lasted just a few moments, but it's one of those moments that I draw on for inspiration."

Michael inspires others by leading sculpture workshops for children and adults, veterans and seniors, both sighted and visually impaired.

In 1999, Michael was named the Outstanding Disabled Veteran of the Year and received the LIFE Presidential Unsung Hero Award. His sculptures can be seen in museums and public buildings across the United States, in the Vatican, and in the White House.

A Special Fan

Many people like to collect Michael's work, but Michael fondly remembers one special young "collector."

"It was maybe twenty years ago at the Indian Market in Santa Fe. One day there was this little boy who came, and he was looking at my work and I was telling him about it. Next year, he came back and said, 'I was here last year. Do you remember me?' And I said, 'Yes.' He said, 'I want to buy that little buffalo.' And I said, 'OK.' I told him how much it was.

"As he paid for it, he said, 'I worked all last summer and this summer, and saved my money.' I had no words to describe the emotion I felt. I still can't describe what a moment like that feels like."

Does Michael have one piece of sculpture that is his very favorite? Could it be the buffalo from the Santa Fe Indian Market? Or the bear with a fish in its mouth?

"You know, it's the same as with children," Michael said. "If you have more than one, you love them all equally. That's how I feel about my sculptures."

Using a Rubric

A rubric is a tool that lists "what counts" in a piece of writing. How do you use a rubric? You assign 1, 2, 3, or 4 points to describe how well the author handled certain writing tasks.

Remember the questions you read on page 74? Those questions were used to make this rubric.

"Hi! I'm Eva. What did you think of the summary on page 75? Well, we're going to evaluate it using this rubric. First, we have to read the questions and the scoring information for each question. After we assess that summary, I'm going to write my own summary of an article. I'll use the rubric and the model to help me. You can do the same."

Audience

Does the writer state the topic in the first sentence so the reader knows what the summary is about?

Organization

Does the writer organize the main points in a logical way?

Elaboration

Does the writer include only the important details?

Clarification

Does the writer avoid using wordy phrases and sentences?

Conventions & Skills

Do the subject and verb of each sentence agree?

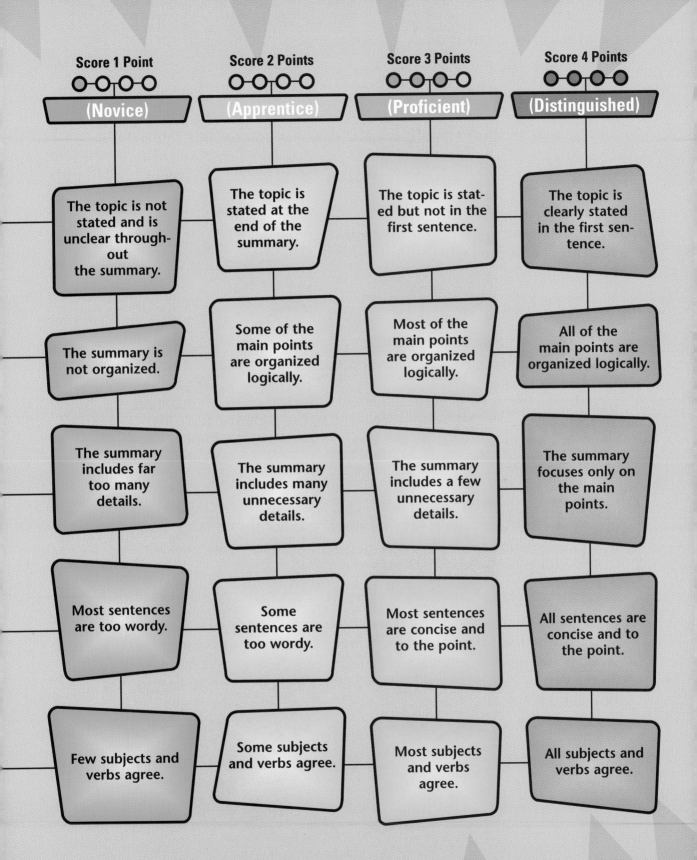

Score 1 Point (Novice)	Score 2 Points (Apprentice)	Score 3 Points (Proficient)	Score 4 Points (Distinguished)
The topic is not stated and is unclear throughout the summary.	The topic is stated at the end of the summary.	The topic is stated but not in the first sentence.	The topic is clearly stated in the first sentence.
The summary is not organized.	Some of the main points are organized logically.	Most of the main points are organized logically.	All of the main points are organized logically.
The summary includes far too many details.	The summary includes many unnecessary details.	The summary includes a few unnecessary details.	The summary focuses only on the main points.
Most sentences are too wordy.	Some sentences are too wordy.	Most sentences are concise and to the point.	All sentences are concise and to the point.
Few subjects and verbs agree.	Some subjects and verbs agree.	Most subjects and verbs agree.	All subjects and verbs agree.

Using a Rubric to Study the Model

Use the rubric to evaluate Keesha Kane's summary. Discuss each question on the rubric with your classmates. Find words and sentences in the summary that help you answer each one.

Audience

Does the writer state the topic in the first sentence so the reader knows what the summary is about?

" The topic of the article—and the summary—is Michael Naranjo, a Native American sculptor. Did you notice how the writer told the audience the topic in her very first sentence? "

Michael Naranjo is a Native American sculptor in Santa Fe, New Mexico. He chose his career when he was a boy helping his mother make pottery in the pueblo. At age 23, however, Naranjo was wounded in the Vietnam War. He was blinded and left without the complete use of one hand.

Does the writer organize the main points in a logical way?

66 The writer follows the organization of the article in her summary. After she tells the topic, she explains how Naranjo deals with his disability. In this paragraph, she summarizes how Naranjo got over his fear that he couldn't be a sculptor. 99

Naranjo was unsure if he would still be able to sculpt. While recovering in the hospital, he molded several clay sculptures of animals. One was so good that it was photographed for the newspaper. That convinced him to pursue his dream.

Does the writer include only the important details?

66 The summary is short, but I think the writer still includes all the main points. She even tells how successful the sculptor is. See how she does it? It's nice and brief.

Naranjo has won awards for his work and leads sculpture workshops. His sculptures are displayed in museums and public buildings around the world. Private collectors also seek his art.

66 The article includes details about how the sculptor mixed his mother's clay. It also tells about a little boy who saved money to buy a sculpture. The writer knew those were not main points, so she left them out. 99

Clarification

Does the writer avoid using wordy phrases and sentences?

> This writer knows that a summary needs to be as short as possible, so she made sure her writing was not wordy. For the second sentence below, she might have written, "He sits and thinks about the image in his mind. After he gets a picture of it, the image goes to his fingertips." Instead, she carefully chose her words and used as few of them as possible.

Although he cannot see, he can remember images from his past. His mind carries the images to his fingertips.

Conventions & Skills

Do the subject and verb of each sentence agree?

> The subjects and their verbs definitely agree. Take the second sentence above, the one I was just telling you about. **His mind** is a singular subject, so it needs the singular verb **carries.** She did it just right.

Now it's my turn to write!

Here I go! I'm going to write my own summary using good writing strategies. I'll use what I learned from the rubric and the model. Follow along with me and watch how I do it.

Eva

Writer of a Summary

Name:	Eva
Home:	Connecticut
Hobbies:	coin collecting, planting trees, Connecticut history
Favorite Tree:	white oak (Connecticut's state tree)
Favorite Book:	*A Gathering of Days: A New England Girl's Journal, 1830–32* by Joan Blos
Assignment:	summary

66 My teacher asked us to write a summary of an article. I chose the article that starts below because it combines my interests in trees, the history of my state, and coins. As you read the article, identify the main points in it. On page 86, you will see the notes I took as I read it. 99

The Tree That Saved History

by Jane Sutcliffe

An unusual funeral took place in Hartford, Connecticut, on August 21, 1856. The city's bells tolled in mourning, and a band played funeral hymns. It was an outpouring of grief fit for a hero—except that this hero was a tree, a white oak to be exact.

For nearly 169 years this special tree had been known simply as the Charter Oak in honor of the part it played in the history of colonial America.

The Charter Oak was an old and respected tree even before colonial times. Native Americans of the area held meetings under its branches. And when the tree's new leaves were as big as a mouse's ear, they knew that it was time to plant corn.

In time, the English came to the valley surrounding the big oak. They settled there and founded the colony of Connecticut. Every colony had to obtain a contract, called a charter, from the king of England. The charter helped to protect the colony's rights. The charter given to Connecticut by King Charles II in 1662 was the pride of the colony. It allowed the colonists to govern themselves by their own constitution. More than a century before the Declaration of Independence, the charter treated Connecticut almost as if it were an independent country.

Then, in 1685, King Charles died. The new English ruler, King James II, not only disapproved of Connecticut's charter but he also disliked having so many colonies. He thought it would be better to combine the colonies of the northeast into one big colony.

King James ordered Sir Edmund Andros, the governor of the Dominion of New England, to seize any documents recognizing the colonies' old rights. Most colonies felt they had no choice and turned over their charters. Only Connecticut delayed. Again and again, Andros demanded that Connecticut give up its charter to him. Again and again, the colonists politely but firmly refused. Finally, Andros had had enough. On All Hallow's Eve, 1687, Andros and more than sixty British soldiers marched into Hartford.

Connecticut Governor Robert Treat was waiting for Andros at the door of the meeting-house, where leaders of the colony were assembled. Politely he escorted Andros inside. Andros wasted no time. He demanded that Connecticut obey the king and surrender its charter.

By now a crowd of townspeople had gathered outside. As they strained to hear every word, Governor Treat spoke passionately about the struggles of the people to build their colony, and about their love of freedom. Giving up the charter, he said, would be like giving up his life. Andros was unmoved. At dark, candles were lit so that the meeting could continue, but Andros had heard enough. He demanded to see the charter. The colonists could delay no longer. They brought out the charter and placed it on the table before him.

Suddenly all the candles in the room went out. In the darkness, a young patriot, Captain Joseph Wadsworth, snatched the charter and jumped out an open window. Carefully wrapping the document in his cloak, he placed it in the hollow of the great white oak. Had the brave captain simply seized the opportunity provided by the sudden darkness, or had it all been a clever plan? No one would ever know. By the time the candles were lit again, Andros was looking at nothing but innocent faces.

If Andros was furious at being outsmarted, he did not show it. With or without the charter, he said that the government of the colony was over. Fortunately, King James was soon

> *Captain Joseph Wadsworth carefully placed Connecticut's charter in the hollow of the great white oak.*

overthrown. Andros was imprisoned and then sent back to England. The new rulers, King William III and Queen Mary II, agreed that since Connecticut had never surrendered its charter, the colony could take up its old freedoms again.

The Charter Oak became a beloved symbol of freedom throughout the land. After it was blown down in a storm on August 21, 1856, people requested keepsakes of its wood. There was plenty to go around—so much, in fact, that author Mark Twain said there was enough "to build a plank road from here (Hartford) to Great Salt Lake City."

Craftsmen fashioned pianos, chairs, and even a cradle of Charter Oak wood. One of the fanciest pieces was an elaborately carved chair that is still used in the Senate Chamber in the State Capitol Building in Hartford. It occupies a place of honor in memory of the Charter Oak, one of the most unusual heroes in our country's struggle for liberty.

The Charter Oak appears on the Connecticut quarter, issued in 1999 by the U.S. Mint. Connecticut became a state in 1788.

Prewriting

Gather
Read an article and take notes on the main points.

"Here are my notes from the article. Did you choose the same main points?"

Notes on "The Tree That Saved History"

- Charter Oak grew in Hartford, CT, important in CT's history. Funeral held for tree.

- English settlers who founded CT colony got charter (contract) from King Charles II to govern themselves. King Charles II died. New king (James II) wanted to take charter away.

- Edmund Andros (gov. of New England) tried to collect CT charter. Met with CT gov. and other leaders in Hartford. When candles went out, Captain Joseph Wadsworth grabbed charter and jumped through window. He hid the charter in a huge white oak.

- King James took CT freedom anyway. New king and queen said CT didn't give up charter so it got its freedom back.

- Tree became symbol of freedom: Wood made into fancy chair. Tree is on CT state quarter.

Go to page 42 in the **Practice** the Strategy **Notebook!**

Prewriting

Organize

Use my notes to make a spider map.

❝I need to make sure my information is well organized. I'll start by organizing my notes into a spider map. Each leg of my spider will be a main point about the Charter Oak.

"You can see my spider map below.❞

Spider Map

A **spider map** organizes information about a topic. A main point is written on each leg.

Old white oak was important in history of CT.

Charter Oak symbolizes freedom; chair made from it is still in CT capitol.

Charter Oak of CT

King took CT's freedom anyway, but CT got it back.

King James tried to take away CT's Charter.

Charter was hidden in an old oak tree.

Go to page 46 in the **Practice** the Strategy **Notebook!**

Drafting

Write

Draft my summary. State the topic in the first sentence. Include all the main points from the article.

" It's time to start writing! The **Rubric** reminds me that the audience just needs main points. My classmates are my audience. They will be glad if I don't ramble on about the details.

"I'll start with the topic of my article. My teacher said that most summaries are only about one-third or less as long as the original article. That guideline will help me keep my summary short.

"When I write this first draft of my summary, I will do my best with spelling and grammar. I can correct any errors I make later.

"I wrote a paragraph or two about each main point, but after I read my first draft, I realized I forgot a main point. I'll squeeze it in. "

topic ———→ **The Charter Oak**   [ist DRAFT]

The Charter Oak was important in the history of Connecticut. This tree even had a funeral.

main points → In colonal times, England's King Charles II granted charters to the American colonies that he ruled in those days before they were part of the United States. The charters from the king was contracts that gave the colonies the freedom to govern themselves instead of having Great Britain govern them. Connecticut got its charter in 1662. In 1685, 23 years later, after King Charles II died, King James II said to collect the charters and join all the New England colonies into one. Edmund Andros, the govenor of New England, got all the charters except Connecticut's.

~~Then he~~ Andros went to Hartford, Connecticut, to ask for the charter. He brought 60 British soldiers and met with the colony's governor, Robert Treat, on All Hallow's Eve. Other leaders of the colony was there, too. Before Andros could take the charter, however, the candles in the room blew out. A patriot named Captain Joseph Wadsworth grabbed the charter and leeped out the **main points** window. He wrapped the ~~paper~~ ^charter in his cloak and hid it in an old white oak tree.

added main point — King James II didn't get the charter, but he took away Connecticut's freedom anyway.

^Soon another English king and queen came into power. They ~~said~~ ^ruled that the colony could have its freedom back because it never ~~gave~~ ^surrendered ~~up~~ its charter.

~~We don't~~ In 1856 a storm blew down the tree. After a funeral for the Charter Oak, its wood was made into a fancy chair. It sit in a place of honor in the state capitol building in Hartford. The Charter Oak appears on the 1999 Connecticut state quarter. It ^now symbolizes our freedom.

Go to page 47 in the **Practice** ^the Strategy **Notebook!**

Revising

Elaborate

Make sure I have included only important details.

> When I checked the **Rubric** again, I noticed that it says to include only important details. That's when I realized that I had added too many unnecessary details to my summary. Do you see all the details I crossed out below? When you write a summary, the idea is to omit unnecessary details, not add them!

[2nd DRAFT]

Andros went to Hartford, Connecticut, to ask for the charter. He ~~brought 60 British soldiers and~~ met with the colony's governor, ~~Robert Treat, on All Hallow's Eve.~~ Other leaders of the colony was there, too. Before Andros could take the charter, however, the candles in the room blew out. A patriot named ~~Captain~~ Joseph Wadsworth grabbed the charter and leeped out the window. He ~~wrapped the charter in his cloak and~~ hid ~~it~~ the charter in an old white oak tree.

deleted details

Go to page 49 in the **Practice** the Strategy **Notebook!**

Revising

Clarify — Take out wordy phrases and sentences.

" If you want a piece of writing to be short, you have to get rid of any extra words. I read my paper aloud to myself to listen for wordy phrases and sentences. I heard a lot of extra words! I got rid of them in this paragraph and in a few other paragraphs, too. Do you see any extra words I missed? "

READ TO MYSELF

Wordy Sentence

A **wordy sentence** uses too many words to explain something. It may explain something readers already know or do not need to know. It may repeat something that was explained earlier.

[3rd DRAFT]

wordy

In colonal times, England's King Charles II granted charters to the American colonies ~~that he ruled in those days before they were part of the United States.~~ The charters from the king was contracts that gave the colonies the freedom to govern themselves ~~instead of having Great Britain govern them.~~ Connecticut gained its charter in 1662. In 1685, ~~23 years later,~~ after King Charles II died, King James II ~~said~~ to collect the charters. Edmund Andros, the govenor of New England, ~~got all~~ the charters except Connecticut's.

gave orders

seized

Go to page 50 in the **Practice** the Strategy **Notebook!**

Editing

Proofread
Check to see that the subject and verb of each sentence agree.

“I have a little trouble with subject-verb agreement. Now is the time for me to find and fix any mistakes I've made. It's also the time to fix any other errors I made in spelling, grammar, or punctuation.”

Subject-Verb Agreement

A **singular subject** requires a **singular verb,** and a **plural subject** requires a **plural verb**.

In many sentences, a prepositional phrase comes between the subject and the verb. In the example below, *colony* is the object of the preposition *of*.

Example: Other leaders *of the colony* were there.

Do not mistake the object of the preposition for the subject of the sentence. The verb must match the subject of the sentence, not the object of the preposition (op).

Incorrect: States in the East views the Charter Oak as a symbol of liberty.

Correct: States in the East view the Charter Oak as a symbol of liberty.

Incorrect: The tallest of the white oaks are 80 feet high.

Correct: The tallest of the white oaks is 80 feet high.

Extra Practice
See **Subject-Verb Agreement** (pages CS 8–CS 9) in the back of this book.

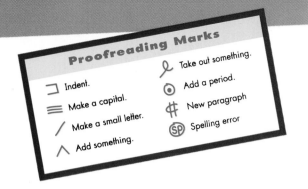

Proofreading Marks

⌐ Indent.

≡ Make a capital.

/ Make a small letter.

∧ Add something.

⌐ Take out something.

⊙ Add a period.

⌗ New paragraph

SP Spelling error

"Here's most of my fourth draft, so you can see the kinds of errors I corrected."

"The Tree That Saved History" by Jane Sutcliffe   [4th DRAFT]

Summary by Eva

The Charter Oak was important in the history of Connecticut. This tree even had a funeral.

In colonial times, England's King Charles II granted charters to the American colonies. The charters from the king was contracts [were] that gave the colonies the freedom to govern themselves. Connecticut gained its charter in 1662. After King Charles II died in 1685, King James II gave orders to collect the charters and combine all New England colonies into one. Edmund Andros, the govenor of New England, seized all the charters except Connecticut's.

Andros went to Hartford, Connecticut, to demand the charter. He met with the colony's governor. Other leaders of the colony was there, too. Before Andros could take the charter, however, the candles in the room blew out. In the darkness, a patriot named Joseph Wadsworth grabbed the charter and leeped out the window. He hid the charter in the hollow of an old white oak tree.

correct subject-verb agreement

Go to page 51 in the **Practice the Strategy Notebook!**

Publishing

Share — **Read my summary to the class.**

> **Name:** Eva
> **Assignment:** summary
> **Topic:** the Charter Oak
> **Audience:** classmates
> **Method of Publication:** oral reading
> **Reason for Choice:** The class is reading aloud summaries of articles about our state.

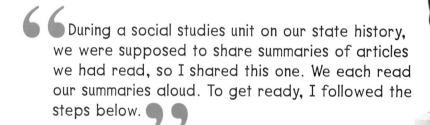

" During a social studies unit on our state history, we were supposed to share summaries of articles we had read, so I shared this one. We each read our summaries aloud. To get ready, I followed the steps below. "

1. First, I checked my summary one more time for mistakes.

2. I made a clean copy of my summary.

3. Next, I practiced reading my summary aloud several times. That way, I knew it so well that I could look up a few times while I read.

4. Then I prepared a short introduction that told the name of the article, its author, where it was published, and when.

5. I read my summary aloud to the class.

"The Tree That Saved History" by Jane Sutcliffe

Summary by Eva

The Charter Oak was important in the history of Connecticut. This tree even had a funeral.

In colonial times, England's King Charles II granted charters to the American colonies. The charters were contracts that gave the colonies the freedom to govern themselves. Connecticut gained its charter in 1662. After King Charles II died in 1685, King James II gave orders to collect the charters and combine all New England colonies into one. Edmund Andros, governor of New England, seized all the charters except Connecticut's.

Andros went to Hartford, Connecticut, to demand the charter. He met with the colony's governor and other leaders. Before Andros could take the charter, however, the candles in the room blew out. In the darkness, a patriot named Joseph Wadsworth grabbed the charter and leaped out the window. He hid the charter in the hollow of an old white oak tree.

King James II didn't get the charter, but he took away Connecticut's freedom anyway. Soon another English king and queen came into power. They ruled that the colony could have its freedom back because it never surrendered its charter.

In 1856 a storm blew down the tree. After a funeral for the Charter Oak, its wood was carved into many things. A beautiful chair made from the Charter Oak now sits in the state capitol. The Charter Oak also appears on the 1999 Connecticut state quarter.

USING the Rubic for Assessment

Go to page 52 in the **Practice Notebook!** the Strategy Use that rubric to assess Eva's paper. Try using the rubric to assess your own writing.

your own EXPOSITORY writing

Health

Put the strategies you practiced in this unit to work to write your own business letter, summary, or both! You can:

- develop the writing you did in the Your Own Writing pages of the *Practice the Strategy Notebook*;

- pick an idea below and write something new;

- choose another idea of your own.

Be sure to follow the steps in the writing process. Use the rubrics in this unit to assess your writing.

Business Letter

- to an art store about nontoxic art supplies
- to a sports facility about a service it provides
- to a coach about promoting safety in sports
- to the author of a book about a health topic

Summary

- of a Web site about the food groups
- of a brochure about how to handle allergies or stress
- of an article about the Special Olympics
- of a book chapter on camping safety

portfolio

School–Home Connection

Keep a writing portfolio. Think about adding the activities from the *Practice the Strategy Notebook* to your writing portfolio. You may want to take your portfolio home to share.

PeRSuASiVe
writing
convinces the reader to do something.

1
Book Review

2
Persuasive Essay

PERSUASIVE writing

Book Review

In this chapter, you will work with one kind of persuasive writing: a **book review**.

A **book review** expresses the writer's opinion about a book. The opinion is then supported with examples and details from the book. A book review is also persuasive because it tries to convince readers that the writer's opinion about the book is correct.

The book review on the next page follows a compare-and-contrast format. It examines the similarities and differences between two books. Read these questions. Then read the review, keeping the questions in mind.

 Does the writer clearly express his or her opinion to the reader and support this opinion convincingly?

 Does the writer organize the review so the comparisons are clear?

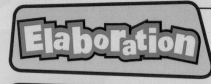 Does the writer use facts, examples, and quotations to support the comparisons?

 Does the writer use signal words to make the similarities and differences clear?

 Does the writer avoid using dependent clauses as sentences?

Two Books by One Excellent Author

by Juan Perro

Virginia Hamilton has written a wide range of stories. *The House of Dies Drear*, for example, is a spellbinding mystery. In contrast, *Cousins* is an emotional story of love and betrayal. Although different, both books are ideal for middle graders.

These readers can easily identify with the young main characters in these two books. While these characters are both independent, they love their families. In *The House of Dies Drear*, Thomas Small attempts to unravel the dark secrets of his new house by himself. Thomas wants to prove that he is brave and smart, like his father. He also wants to protect his family from dangers in the house. In *Cousins*, on the other hand, young Cammy loves being her mother's "baby." Like Thomas, though, she also enjoys freedom. She wants to visit her grandmother whenever she pleases. Unlike Thomas, Cammy rarely sees her father. Instead, she looks up to her big brother. Sometimes she feels "like she would burst with love" for him.

The settings of both books combine the familiar and the unfamiliar. Thomas's new home is a mysterious old house. The huge mansion had been a stop on the Underground Railroad. It has a homey kitchen, but it also has secret passages. The house looms over the story, creating a dark mood. In contrast, the pleasant little town in *Cousins* creates a sunny mood. As in *The House of Dies Drear*, however, that setting can turn threatening. In *Cousins*, a river swallows one of Cammy's cousins.

Each book addresses the theme of dealing with changes. Many middle-grade readers can identify with this theme, as they are also dealing with changes. Thomas has to overcome his fears about moving to a new place. Similarly, Cammy copes with her grief over the death of her cousin.

Virginia Hamilton tells stories that middle graders can understand and enjoy. Read *The House of Dies Drear*, *Cousins*, or any of Hamilton's other novels. You will see how the characters, settings, and themes make her stories so appealing.

Using a **Rubric**

A rubric is a tool that describes "what counts" for a piece of writing. You assign 1, 2, 3, or 4 points to tell how well the author handled certain writing tasks. A rubric can also help a writer know what aspects of writing to focus on in writing a book review.

Remember the questions you read on page 98? Those questions were used to make this rubric.

> " Hey there! I'm Rachel. Did you think the book review on page 99 was convincing? Let's use this rubric to assess it. First, we have to read these questions and the information for each question. Then we'll be ready to assess the review. After we finish evaluating that book review, I'm going to write my own. You can write one, too. "

Audience

Does the writer clearly express his or her opinion to the reader and support this opinion convincingly?

Organization

Does the writer organize the review so the comparisons are clear?

Elaboration

Does the writer use facts, examples, and quotations to support the comparisons?

Clarification

Does the writer use signal words to make the similarities and differences clear?

Conventions & Skills

Does the writer avoid using dependent clauses as sentences?

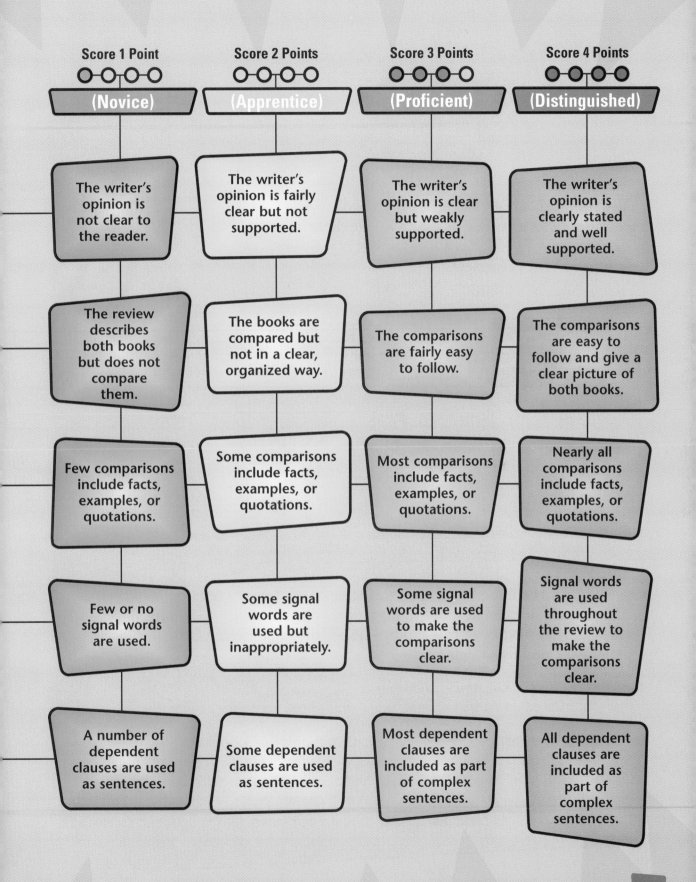

Score 1 Point

(Novice)

The writer's opinion is not clear to the reader.

The review describes both books but does not compare them.

Few comparisons include facts, examples, or quotations.

Few or no signal words are used.

A number of dependent clauses are used as sentences.

Score 2 Points

(Apprentice)

The writer's opinion is fairly clear but not supported.

The books are compared but not in a clear, organized way.

Some comparisons include facts, examples, or quotations.

Some signal words are used but inappropriately.

Some dependent clauses are used as sentences.

Score 3 Points

(Proficient)

The writer's opinion is clear but weakly supported.

The comparisons are fairly easy to follow.

Most comparisons include facts, examples, or quotations.

Some signal words are used to make the comparisons clear.

Most dependent clauses are included as part of complex sentences.

Score 4 Points

(Distinguished)

The writer's opinion is clearly stated and well supported.

The comparisons are easy to follow and give a clear picture of both books.

Nearly all comparisons include facts, examples, or quotations.

Signal words are used throughout the review to make the comparisons clear.

All dependent clauses are included as part of complex sentences.

Using a Rubric

to Study the Model

Use the rubric to evaluate Juan Perro's book review in each category. Discuss each question on the rubric with your classmates. Find words and sentences in the story that support your assessment.

Audience

Does the writer clearly express his or her opinion to the reader and support this opinion convincingly?

66 The writer leads up to his opinion, which my teacher told us is also called a 'thesis statement.' First, he points out that Virginia Hamilton has written many books. Next, he names two of them. Then he clearly states his opinion that middle graders should read these two. 99

Virginia Hamilton has written a wide range of stories. *The House of Dies Drear,* for example, is a spellbinding mystery. In contrast, *Cousins* is an emotional story of love and betrayal. Although different, both books are ideal for middle graders.

66 The rest of the review supports the writer's opinion. He explains how each book appeals to young people with its characters, setting, and theme. The comparisons are interesting, and they don't tell too much. They made me want to read the books to find out more. 99

Does the writer organize the review so the comparisons are clear?

❝ The writer organized his comparisons in a very clear way. He focuses on the books' characters, settings, and themes. First, he states a way both books appeal to readers. Then he demonstrates how each book does that. He always discusses <u>The House of Dies Drear</u> first and then <u>Cousins</u> so you can keep the comparisons straight. Read this paragraph to see what I mean. ❞

Each book addresses the theme of dealing with changes. Many middle-grade readers can identify with this theme, as they are also dealing with changes. Thomas has to overcome his fears about moving to a new place. Similarly, Cammy copes with her grief over the death of her cousin.

Does the writer use facts, examples, and quotations to support the comparisons?

❝ I noticed that the writer uses examples from the books to support his comparisons of the characters, settings, and themes. In this paragraph about the characters, he also uses a quotation from one of the books. That makes the comparison more interesting, too. ❞

In *The House of Dies Drear,* Thomas Small attempts to unravel the dark secrets of his new house by himself. Thomas wants to prove that he is brave and smart, like his father. He also wants to protect his family from dangers in the house. In *Cousins,* on the other hand, young Cammy loves being her mother's "baby." Like Thomas, though, she also enjoys freedom. She wants to visit her grandmother whenever she pleases. Unlike Thomas, Cammy rarely sees her father. Instead, she looks up to her big brother. Sometimes she feels "like she would burst with love" for him.

Clarification

Does the writer use signal words to make the similarities and differences clear?

"The writer uses quite a few signal words to make sure you know he's comparing and contrasting one thing with another. In these two sentences, he's comparing how the setting creates the mood in each book. Do you see how he uses the signal words **In contrast** to make the comparisons clear?"

The house looms over the story, creating a dark mood. In contrast, the pleasant little town in *Cousins* creates a sunny mood.

Conventions & SKiLLS

Does the writer avoid using dependent clauses as sentences?

"I didn't find any dependent clauses used as sentences. That would be a grammar error! This sentence, for example, begins with a dependent clause, but the clause is part of a complex sentence. That makes it OK!"

While these characters are both independent, they love their families.

 Now it's my turn to write!

How can I apply good writing strategies in my own book review? Just watch! I'm going to use what I learned from the model and the rubric. "

RacHeL

Writer of a Book Review

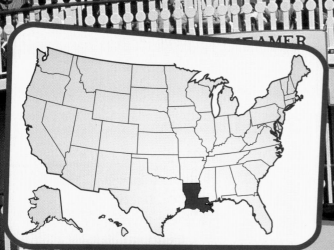

Name:	Rachel
Home:	Louisiana
Hobbies:	sailing, collecting stuffed rabbits
Prized Possession:	a necklace my grandmother brought with her when she came to America during World War II
Assignment:	compare-and-contrast book review

PrewRiting

Gather

Think about a book I liked and find another book that is similar yet different. Jot notes about the first book. Keep a response journal as I read the new book.

"Recently, I read Number the Stars by Lois Lowry. I chose it because it was about my Jewish heritage. I wanted to find a book kind of like that to use for my next writing assignment: a book review that compares two novels. The review on page 99 compares two books by the same author. I thought about doing that, using another book by Lois Lowry. I also considered comparing a fiction and a nonfiction book on the same topic.

"In the end, I decided to compare two fiction books on the same topic by different authors. Our school librarian suggested Good Night, Maman. It's a fiction book about my Jewish heritage, like Number the Stars, but it's by a different author, Norma Fox Mazer.

"To start my book review, I wrote these notes from memory about Number the Stars before I read Good Night, Maman."

My Notes on Number the Stars

★ World War II: Nazi soldiers all over Copenhagen, Denmark

★ 1943: Nazis begin arresting Jews. Jewish Rosens leave their daughter Ellen with her friend Annemarie Johansen and her family. Johansens pretend Ellen is their daughter.

★ Annemarie and her mom take Ellen to Uncle Henrik's house at the coast. Ellen's parents come there. They have a fake funeral so Jews can gather at house disguised as mourners. Nazis investigate; girls are terrified, but brave.

★ Annemarie's parents, Uncle Henrik, and others help Jews hide on fishing boats to escape to Sweden.

★ Annemarie meets Nazis in woods; she is frightened, but brave. Rosens get to Sweden safely.

"Instead of taking notes as I read my second book, I decided to keep a response journal. That way, I could jot down my thoughts as I read the book. This book is also about a Jewish girl and her family hiding from the Nazis during World War II. I included my own reactions and lots of quotations (with the page numbers where I found them). You can read the first part of my response journal below. It will remind me about the plot, theme, setting, and characters and help me find good quotes to use in my review."

Response Journal

A **response journal** is a notebook or other place where someone jots down his or her impressions about an experience, such as reading a book.

My Response Journal for Good Night, Maman
(page 1)

I couldn't stay quiet for a year like Karin Levi did in that attic closet. I guess she just had to.

Maman is strict but sweet. You can see why Karin loves her so much. Marc acts so mature. He's trying to be the man since his dad was shot.

It must have been terrible to run from your home, begging for food, with no place to live. Karin said, "It had been weeks since I'd slept on a real bed, in a real room." (p. 31) She said, "We were free and unfree. We were in our own beloved land, but it was not ours." (p. 36)

It was so sad when Karin kissed Maman goodbye. Karin was worried Maman wouldn't find them after she got better. "How was she going to do that? Find us where?" Karin said. (p. 58)

I thought everyone who helped the Jews was nice to them, but Madame Zetain wasn't. The farmer and Maria Theresa were. Maria Theresa even told them about a ship that could take them to America.

Go to page 54 in the **Practice** the Strategy **Notebook!**

Prewriting

Organize

Use my notes and response journal to make a Venn diagram.

> The **Rubric** stresses the importance of organizing my book review. I'll review my notes and my response journal and organize the important points into a Venn diagram. This diagram will help me figure out how the books are similar and different.

Venn Diagram

A **Venn diagram** is two overlapping circles that show how two things are similar and different. Ways the things are similar are described in the overlapping section. Ways they are different are described in the outside part of each circle.

> One of the first things I notice is that Number the Stars is set in Denmark, but Good Night, Maman is set in France and other countries. That's one way the two books are different. I'll put that information in each outside circle.
>
> "However, both books take place during World War II. That's one way they are the same. I'll write that in the overlapping part of the circles. I already have a good start on my Venn diagram!

“Here is my completed Venn diagram. Besides the settings, I compared the characters, the main events, and the themes. I decided that the themes are the same: Hope and bravery help the children survive. **”**

Venn Diagram
Comparing My Books

Number the Stars

- set in Denmark
- Annemarie and Ellen are warm and fed.
- Rosens are together and safe.
- Rosens escape to Sweden.

Both Books

- 10-year-old girls
- set in WWII
- Nazis are searching for Jews.
- People help Jews escape.
- Hope and bravery help the children survive.

Good Night, Maman

- set in France, Italy, USA
- Karin and Marc are homeless and hungry.
- Levi family splits up; mother dies later.
- Karin and Marc escape to USA.

Go to page 58 in the **Practice** the Strategy **Notebook!**

Persuasive Writing • Book Review   **109**

Drafting

Write
Draft my book review. Start by writing my opinion or thesis statement.

> The **Rubric** points out that my opinion or thesis statement should be clear to my audience. My classmates are my audience, so I'll state my opinion about the books in a way that will be clear to my readers.
>
> "So what is my thesis statement or opinion of these two books? The writer who reviewed Virginia Hamilton's books seemed to like both books about the same. Her thesis statement was that both books are good for middle graders.
>
> "After looking at my notes and response journal, I think I like Good Night, Maman better than Number the Stars. That will be my thesis statement!
>
> "Next, I'll summarize the plot of Number the Stars and the plot of Good Night, Maman. Then I'll point out ways they are the same and different. I'll show why Good Night, Maman is better in some ways, so my comparisons support my thesis statement."

Thesis Statement

A **thesis statement** is the opinion the writer is attempting to prove. The writer tries to convince readers to accept or believe his or her opinion or thesis statement.

66 Here is part of my first draft. 99

thesis statement

Bravery and Hope

Number the Stars by Lois Lowry and Good Night, Maman by Norma Fox Mazer tell about brave young girls during World War II. ~~In~~ I prefer Good Night, Maman. It shows better than Number the Stars that children needed both hope and bravery to get through terrible experiences during the war.

In Number the Stars, Annemarie Johansen and Ellen Rosen are friends. They are 10 years old and live in Copenhagen, Denmark. It is 1943, and the Nazis have started arresting Jews in Copenhagen. The Rosens are Jewish.

Ellen stays with Annemarie and pretends to be her sister. Although scared, Annemarie and Ellen face the Nazis when they come to the Johansens' apartment.

The Johansens then take Ellen to Uncle Henrik's house by the sea. There Ellen is reunited with her parents. Annemarie realizes her family and friends are in danger, but she is unsure that she is brave enough to help them. Uncle Henrik says, "I think you are like your mama, and your papa, and like me. Frightened, but determined, and if the time came to be brave, I am quite sure you would be very, very brave."

Go to page 60 in the **Practice** the Strategy **Notebook!**

Persuasive Writing · Book Review

III

Revising

Elaborate

Check my essay for completeness. Add facts, examples, or quotations to support my comparisons.

" After I wrote my second draft, I had my friend Ariel read it. She didn't think my comparisons were complete enough. I agreed. That's why I added an example and quotations to these paragraphs. They made my comparisons clearer, don't you think? I added more facts, examples, and quotations to other paragraphs in my review, too. "

READ TO A PARTNER

Fact, Example, Quotation

A **fact** is a statement that can be proven to be true.

An **example** is something that helps explain an idea or thought. (Cats and dogs are both examples of pets.)

A **quotation** is the exact words of a speaker or writer.

---

added example and quotation

added quotation

[2nd DRAFT]

Suddenly, the Levis must flee Paris. Annemarie and Ellen see Nazis. Karin's family doesn't. The threat of capture out in the open is always there for the Levis. They must travel at night and hide during the day. Karin is frightened and puzzled. ∧

Karin's journey to freedom is rough. ∧

She does not have food and shelter like Annemarie and Ellen. When Karin's family stops to beg for food at a farmhouse and she sees a cot in the corner, she says, "It had been weeks since I'd slept on a real bed, in a real room."

As they walk, she says, "We were free and unfree. We were in our own beloved land, but it was not ours."

Go to page 61 in the **Practice** the Strategy **Notebook!**

Persuasive Writing · Book Review

Revising

Clarify
Add signal words to make my comparisons clearer.

" The **Rubric** points out that signal words can help make comparisons clearer. My teacher gave us a list of signal words for a compare-and-contrast essay. They include **in the same way, similarly, likewise, like, as, also, on the other hand, in contrast, unlike, although, more/less, yet,** and **but**. I added a few signal words to this paragraph. Read what I wrote to see if it's clearer. *"*

Signal Words

Signal words show how two ideas relate to each other. In compare-and-contrast essays, signal words help tell the reader that two ideas are similar or different.

[3rd DRAFT]

added signal word → Similarly,

Danish people help the Jews in Number the Stars. French and

Italian people help them in Good Night, Maman. In Number the Stars,

In contrast,

Ellen is separated from her parents only for a few days. Karin and

Marc are separated from Maman for months.

added signal words

Go to page 62 in the **Practice** the Strategy **Notebook!**

Editing

Proofread

Check to see that all dependent clauses are part of complex sentences.

" Now it's time to check my draft for mistakes in spelling, capitalization, and punctuation. I need to check another problem, too. Sometimes I use dependent clauses as sentences. They aren't really sentences—they're fragments. I'll make sure they are part of complex sentences. "

Complex Sentences

A **complex sentence** contains an independent clause and a dependent clause. An **independent clause** has a subject and a verb. It is also a simple sentence. A **dependent clause** has a subject and a verb but does not make sense by itself. It is one kind of **sentence fragment**. Dependent clauses begin with **subordinating conjunctions** such as *although, because, if, as, so, before,* or *when.*

A dependent clause should be combined with an independent clause. That way, you create a complex sentence and avoid using sentence fragments.

Example:

Independent clause:

You will learn about World War II.

Dependent clause (sentence fragment):

When you study history.

Dependent clause + independent clause = complex sentence:

When you study history, you will learn about World War II.

Extra Practice

See **Complex Sentences** (pages CS 10–CS 11) in the back of this book.

Persuasive Writing · Book Review

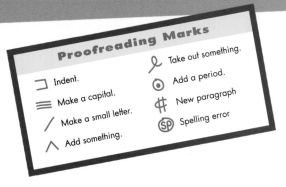

Proofreading Marks

⌐ Indent.

≡ Make a capital.

/ Make a small letter.

∧ Add something.

℘ Take out something.

⊙ Add a period.

New paragraph

SP Spelling error

> " Here's part of my fourth draft, so you can see the kinds of errors I corrected. "

[4th DRAFT]

In the United States, Karin and Marc stay in a refugee camp and learn American ways. Karin still writes to Maman, but she also is determined to make new friends. "It had been years since I'd had friends my own age. I hardly even remembered how to act like a friend, but I pretended I did," Karin says. Although it's not easy , Karin does well. ← being in a new country, Perhaps Ellen does well in Sweden, too, but Number the Stars does not discuss that.

included fragment in a complex sentence

Finally, Karin learns the truth: her mother is dead. Marc has known about it for a few months⊙ he helps Karin handle her greif. SP grief

When the war ends, Annemarie waits for Ellen to come back to Copenhagen. Karin plans to live in California with her aunt. Although Karin has no parents, She has bravery and hope. She says, "I thought about everything I had learned about people—some bad, some good. And I had learned that you can't look back for too long. You just have to keep going."

Go to page 63 in the **Practice** the Strategy ∧ **Notebook!**

Publishing

Share — Publish my essay in the school newspaper.

> Writer: Rachel
> Assignment: book review
> Topic: two books about brave girls during World War II
> Audience: other students
> Method of Publication: school newspaper
> Reason for Choice: Other students might want to read one or both of these books.

" I like to share my opinions about what I read. The school newspaper seemed like the best place to do that. Here are the steps I followed to get my book review ready to be printed in the newspaper. "

1. To begin, I checked my review one more time for mistakes.

2. I printed a clean copy of it and added my name.

3. Then I submitted my review to the editorial committee of our school newspaper.

Bravery and Hope

by Rachel

Number the Stars by Lois Lowry and Good Night, Maman by Norma Fox Mazer tell about brave young girls during World War II. Good Night, Maman, however, shows better than Number the Stars that children went through terrible experiences during the war and that you need hope, as well as bravery, to get through hardships and move on.

In Number the Stars, Annemarie Johansen and Ellen Rosen are friends. They are 10 years old and live in Copenhagen, Denmark. It is 1943, and the Nazis have started arresting Jews in Copenhagen. The Rosens are Jewish.

Ellen stays with Annemarie and pretends to be her sister. Although scared, Annemarie and Ellen face the Nazis when they come to the Johansens' apartment.

The Johansens then take Ellen to Uncle Henrik's house by the sea. There Ellen is reunited with her parents. Annemarie realizes her family and friends are in danger, but she is unsure that she is brave enough to help them. Uncle Henrik says, "I think you are like your mama, and your papa, and like me. Frightened, but determined, and if the time came to be brave, I am quite sure you would be very, very brave."

Later, Annemarie proves she is brave. She delivers an important package to Uncle Henrik. It is a handkerchief treated to make the Nazi dogs lose their sense of smell. The Rosens make it safely to Sweden on Uncle Henrik's boat because the dogs are unable to smell people hidden on the boat.

The main character in Good Night, Maman is also a 10-year-old girl. Karin Levi lives in Paris, France, with her mother (Maman) and her brother, Marc. The Nazis have also occupied this country and have been searching for Jewish people like the Levis. They have shot Karin's father already. Her family must hide in a tiny attic closet for a year. This is worse than anything Annemarie or Ellen goes through, but Karin stays hopeful.

Suddenly, the Levis must flee Paris. Unlike Annemarie and Ellen, they never encounter any Nazi soldiers. On the other hand, the threat of capture out in the open is always there. They must travel at night and hide during the day. Karin is frightened and puzzled. As they walk, she says, "We were free and unfree. We were in our own beloved land, but it was not ours."

Karin's journey to freedom is rough. She does not have food and shelter like Annemarie and Ellen. When Karin's family stops to beg for food at a farmhouse, she sees a cot in the corner. She says, "It had been weeks since I'd slept on a real bed, in a real room."

Danish people help the Jews in Number the Stars. Similarly, French and Italian people help them in Good Night, Maman. In Number the Stars, Ellen is parted from her parents only for a few days. In contrast, Karin and Marc are separated from Maman for months.

The separation becomes wider when Karin and Marc board a ship taking Jewish refugees to the United States. Annemarie and Ellen can depend on their parents for help, but Karin only has Marc. She begins writing letters to Maman. The letters show how brave and strong she is. In her first letter, she writes, "I never wanted to go so far away from you. I didn't want to get on this boat. But Marc said we wouldn't be safe anywhere in Europe until the war was over, and that you would absolutely want us to do this."

In the United States, Karin and Marc stay in a refugee camp and learn American ways. Karin still writes to Maman, but she also is determined to make new friends. "It had been years since I'd had friends my own age. I hardly even remembered how to act like a friend, but I pretended I did," Karin says. Although it's not easy being in a new country, Karin does well. Perhaps Ellen does well in

Sweden, too, but Number the Stars does not discuss that.

Finally, Karin learns the truth: her mother is dead. Marc has known about it for a few months. He helps Karin handle her grief.

When the war ends, Annemarie waits for Ellen to come back to Copenhagen. Karin plans to live in California with her aunt. Although Karin has no parents, she has bravery and hope. Karin says, "I thought about everything I had learned about people—some bad, some good. And I had learned that you can't look back for too long. You just have to keep going."

Both of these books are about 10-year-old Jewish girls coping with life in countries occupied by the Nazis. While I enjoyed reading both of them, I liked Good Night, Maman a little better because I thought the ending was more realistic. Many Jewish families were separated forever by that war, and Good Night, Maman showed that clearly.

USING the Rubric for Assessment

Go to pages 64–65 in the **Practice** the Strategy **Notebook!** Use that rubric to assess Rachel's paper. Try using the rubric to assess your own writing.

PERSUASIVE
writing

Persuasive Essay

In this chapter, you will work with one kind of persuasive writing: a **persuasive essay**.

A **persuasive essay** expresses the writer's opinion on a topic. It tries to convince readers to agree with the writer's opinion and perhaps act in a certain way. For example, a persuasive essay might try to convince readers to conserve energy in specific ways.

Read these questions. Then read the persuasive essay on the next page, keeping these questions in mind.

 Does the writer begin by clearly expressing his or her opinion to the audience?

 Does the writer organize the essay so opinions are supported with facts?

 Does the writer choose appropriate and convincing facts and reasons to support his or her opinion?

 Does the writer avoid using loaded words?

 Does the writer use pronouns with clear antecedents and make sure that pronouns and their antecedents agree?

The Right Angle on the Triangle

by Arina Zubatova

When you think about the Bermuda Triangle, what comes to your mind? Do you picture mysterious forces, time warps, and the underwater city of Atlantis? That is how some people explain the disappearances of boats and planes in the Bermuda Triangle. However, the dangers there are natural, not supernatural.

The corners of the Bermuda Triangle are Bermuda, Puerto Rico, and Fort Lauderdale, Florida. About 100 boats and planes have disappeared in this region. About 1,000 people have died there in the past century. However, that is only ten people a year, not a high number for such a large area. If this region were especially dangerous, insurance companies would charge higher rates for crafts that pass through it. They do not.

Why did those 100 boats and planes disappear in the Triangle? The causes were natural, not supernatural. In the tropics, sudden storms—even giant waterspouts—can destroy ships and aircraft. The Gulf Stream, a strong ocean current, can pull amateur sailors far off course. In addition, the region has trenches thousands of feet deep. In fact, the deepest trench in the Atlantic Ocean is in the Bermuda Triangle. Remains of boats and planes may be buried in these trenches.

Despite these facts, many accidents in the Bermuda Triangle have been described as mysterious. The 1945 disappearance of five Navy bombers off the coast of Florida was one of them. The planes disappeared during a training flight for rookies. The flight was led by an experienced pilot. However, radio transcripts show that his compass was not working. It caused him to lead the group out to sea instead of toward Florida. Then a storm blew in. The planes vanished, and no wreckage was ever found.

The planes probably ended up far out in the Atlantic. There they ran out of gas and fell into the sea. Sharks took the pilots. A trench swallowed the wreckage. In spite of this logical explanation, this and many other disappearances have been blamed on mysterious forces in the Triangle.

People like a good story. Still, we must not ignore the facts about the Bermuda Triangle. The dangers are real, not supernatural.

Using a Rubric

A rubric is a tool that lists "what counts" for a piece of writing. You assign 1, 2, 3, or 4 points to tell how well the author handled certain writing tasks.

Remember the questions you read on page 120? Those questions were used to make this rubric.

"Hey, I'm Anthony. You read the persuasive essay on page 121, right? We're going to evaluate that essay using this rubric. First, you have to read the questions and the information for each question. After we evaluate this essay, I'm going to write a persuasive essay of my own. I'll use what I learned from the rubric and the model. You can watch how I do it."

Audience

Does the writer begin by clearly expressing his or her opinion to the audience?

Organization

Does the writer organize the essay so opinions are supported with facts?

Elaboration

Does the writer choose appropriate and convincing facts and reasons to support his or her opinion?

Clarification

Does the writer avoid using loaded words?

Conventions & Skills

Does the writer use pronouns with clear antecedents and make sure that pronouns and their antecedents agree?

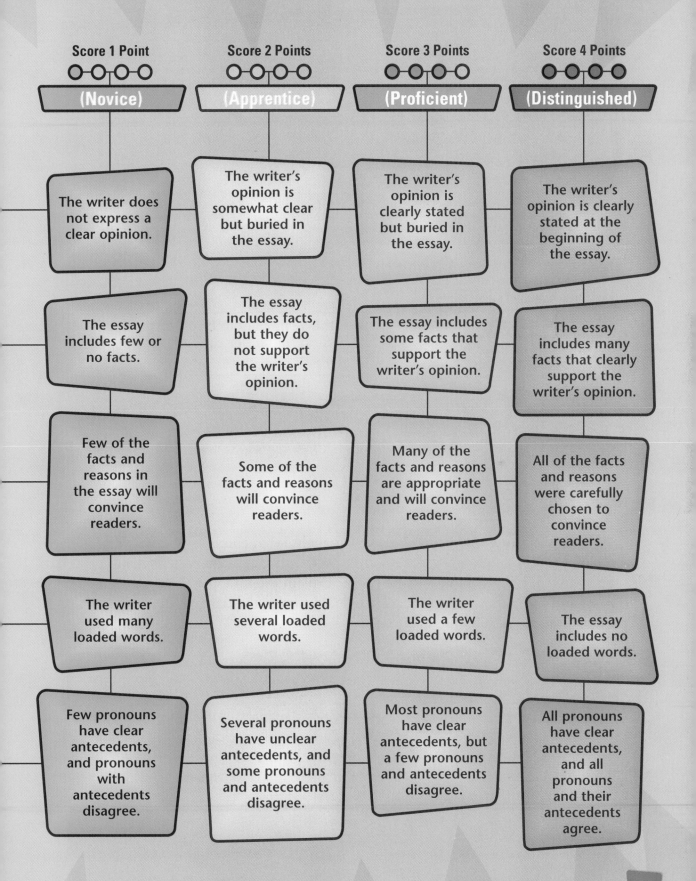

Score 1 Point
(Novice)

Score 2 Points
(Apprentice)

Score 3 Points
(Proficient)

Score 4 Points
(Distinguished)

The writer does not express a clear opinion.

The writer's opinion is somewhat clear but buried in the essay.

The writer's opinion is clearly stated but buried in the essay.

The writer's opinion is clearly stated at the beginning of the essay.

The essay includes few or no facts.

The essay includes facts, but they do not support the writer's opinion.

The essay includes some facts that support the writer's opinion.

The essay includes many facts that clearly support the writer's opinion.

Few of the facts and reasons in the essay will convince readers.

Some of the facts and reasons will convince readers.

Many of the facts and reasons are appropriate and will convince readers.

All of the facts and reasons were carefully chosen to convince readers.

The writer used many loaded words.

The writer used several loaded words.

The writer used a few loaded words.

The essay includes no loaded words.

Few pronouns have clear antecedents, and pronouns with antecedents disagree.

Several pronouns have unclear antecedents, and some pronouns and antecedents disagree.

Most pronouns have clear antecedents, but a few pronouns and antecedents disagree.

All pronouns have clear antecedents, and all pronouns and their antecedents agree.

Using a Rubric
to Study the Model

Discuss each question on the rubric with your classmates. Find words and sentences in the essay that help you answer each one. Use the rubric to evaluate Arina Zubatova's essay on each question.

Does the writer begin by clearly expressing his or her opinion to the audience?

" This writer lets us know her opinion in the very first paragraph. Read the last sentence in the paragraph below again. I really know what she thinks! "

When you think about the Bermuda Triangle, what comes to your mind? Do you picture mysterious forces, time warps, and the underwater city of Atlantis? That is how some people explain the disappearances of boats and planes in the Bermuda Triangle. However, the dangers there are natural, not supernatural.

" Then do you remember how she pointed out that the insurance companies weren't worried about the Bermuda Triangle? Next, she described all the natural dangers in this region, like storms and currents and trenches. By the end of the essay, I was convinced that the causes of the disappearances were natural, not supernatural. "

Does the writer organize the essay so opinions are supported with facts?

> The writer includes a number of facts that helped convince me. First, she explained that there had been 1,000 deaths in the Triangle. Something strange must be going on there, right? Then, though, she pointed out that was an average of only ten deaths each year. That's not very many. Do you remember this part?

The corners of the Bermuda Triangle are Bermuda, Puerto Rico, and Fort Lauderdale, Florida. About 100 boats and planes have disappeared in this region. About 1,000 people have died there in the past century. However, that is only ten people a year, not a high number for such a large area.

Does the writer choose appropriate and convincing facts and reasons to support his or her opinion?

> This writer carefully chose which facts to include. For example, she could have told us the name of the pilot leading the flight, but she didn't. She knew that would not help convince us that the dangers in the Bermuda Triangle are natural. Did you notice how she mentioned the storm, though? It helps to prove that she is right.

Despite these facts, many accidents in the Bermuda Triangle have been described as mysterious. The 1945 disappearance of five Navy bombers off the coast of Florida was one of them. The planes disappeared during a training flight for rookies. The flight was led by an experienced pilot. However, radio transcripts show that his compass was not working. It caused him to lead the group out to sea instead of toward Florida. Then a storm blew in. The planes vanished, and no wreckage was ever found.

Clarification

Does the writer avoid using loaded words?

> The writer might have used loaded, negative words, like **idiot**, to show that she is amazed that some people believe there are mysterious forces in the Bermuda Triangle. However, she doesn't say, 'Some idiots will believe anything.' Instead, she simply says this:

People like a good story. Still, we must not ignore the facts about the Bermuda Triangle. The dangers are real, not supernatural.

Conventions & SKiLLS

Does the writer use pronouns with clear antecedents and make sure that pronouns and their antecedents agree?

> The writer was careful with pronouns. Can you tell what the pronoun **it** refers to in the first sentence below? It refers to **region**, right? **It** and **region** are both singular, so they agree. In the second sentence, **They** is a plural pronoun that refers to **companies**, which is plural, too. She really matched her pronouns.

If this region were especially dangerous, insurance companies would charge higher rates for crafts that pass through it. They do not.

> ## Now it's my turn to write!
> All right! Now I'm going to write a persuasive essay. I'll use what I learned from the rubric and the model. Follow along with me. Here we go!

Anthony

Writer of a Persuasive Essay

Name: Anthony
Home: Oregon
Hobbies: old movies, panning for gold
Favorite Old Movie: *The Treasure of the Sierra Madre* (1948)
Favorite Book: *Ishi* by Louise Jeffredo-Warden
Assignment: persuasive essay

Prewriting

Gather

Choose an issue about which I have an opinion. Find facts to support my opinion and take notes.

" I live in Oregon, but California is the main location of my two favorite hobbies—old movies and gold panning. My favorite aunt lives in California, too, and I go to see her whenever I can.

"Some of my friends say that all Californians are too concerned with how they look and the latest fads. That upsets me. I like Californians. I know that they are as different from each other as the people who live in Oregon.

"When our teacher asked us to write a persuasive essay, I decided to try to convince my classmates that we should not judge people based on where they live. Grouping people like that is called stereotyping. I read some articles about California and stereotyping and took these notes. "

Notes on Stereotyping and Californians

Stereotyping means forming an opinion about people based on their membership in a certain group.

Stereotyping is a kind of prejudice.

CA's population grew 50 percent between 1970 and 1990.

CA has more immigrants from other countries than any other state.

Californians come in all shapes and sizes.

One in four Californians is Hispanic.

In 1990 census, nearly 5 million Californians had German ancestors; 3.5 million were from Irish families.

1990 census: more than half of the people living in CA were not born there.

Migrants come from all over the nation, especially the South and Northeast.

Stereotyping people keeps us from getting to know and understand them.

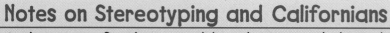

Go to page 66 in the **Practice** the Strategy **Notebook!**

Prewriting

Organize
Use a network tree to organize my ideas.

> I know from the **Rubric** that organization is important. A network tree can help me get my ideas in order. I'll put my opinion at the top, the reasons for it under that, and facts to support each reason underneath it. As I write, I can look at my tree and see which facts support each reason.

Network Tree

A **network tree** organizes information about a topic. The topic or opinion goes at the top, with main ideas or reasons on the next level. The bottom level contains facts to support the main ideas or reasons.

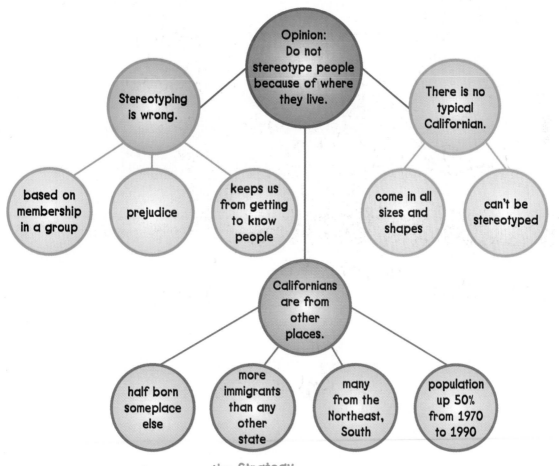

Opinion: Do not stereotype people because of where they live.

- Stereotyping is wrong.
  - based on membership in a group
  - prejudice
  - keeps us from getting to know people
- There is no typical Californian.
  - come in all sizes and shapes
  - can't be stereotyped
- Californians are from other places.
  - half born someplace else
  - more immigrants than any other state
  - many from the Northeast, South
  - population up 50% from 1970 to 1990

Go to page 69 in the **Practice** the Strategy **Notebook!**

Persuasive Writing • Persuasive Essay

129

Write

Draft my essay. State my opinion in the first paragraph and support it with reasons and facts in the following paragraphs. Restate my opinion in the last paragraph.

" As I wrote my first draft, I concentrated on getting my ideas down on paper. I'll do my best with spelling and grammar now. I can fix any mistakes later.

"First, I tried to explain my opinion clearly in my first paragraph. Then I wrote a paragraph for each of my reasons. The **Rubric** reminded me to support my opinions with facts. My network tree helped me do that. At the end of my essay, I stated my opinion again.

"Read my first draft and see if you think my opinion is clear at the beginning and the end. "

Reason, Fact

A **reason** is an explanation behind an act, idea, or argument. For example, a reason to wear a coat outdoors is that it's snowing. A **fact** is a statement that can be proven to be true.

Don't Stereotype States!

[1st DRAFT]

Do you think all Californiains pay way too much attention to how they look? Do you think they all follow the latest fads, no matter how stupid? When we lump people together for some reason, we are stereotyping them. In this case, we are forming an opinion about them based on where they live. That's wrong! The people who

reason supporting
my opinion

live in California are as different from each other as the people

who live in every state. We must stop stereotyping them! ← *my opinion*

Stereotyping is wrong. It's a kind of prejudice. Some ignorant

people use stereotypes to jump to decisions. They decide whether

they like ~~or don't like~~ people because of the group they belong to.

They don't bother to get to know him. It's like being prejudiced

against people because of the shabby clothes they wear or the

strange language she speaks. You could miss meeting ~~nice people~~ if

good friends

you make decisions based on stereotypes.

reason supported
by facts

It's really a dumb mistake to stereotype Californians. In the 1990

census, California had more than 29 million residents. More than half

of Californians were born someplace else, and he moved there.

Between 1970 and 1990, the poplulation of california grew by 50

percent. Many of these new residents came from the northeastern

and southern states. California also has more imigrants from other

countries than any other state. How could you group all these peo-

ple together? How could you say they are all the same?

reason
supported
by facts

There is no typical Californian. One in four Californians is

Hispanic. In the 1990 census, nearly 5 million Californans said he

had German ancestors. Antoher 3.5 million Californians had Irish

ancestors.

Californians have different backgrounds, customs, likes, and dis-

likes. They're just like people everywere. Let's treat Californians

like the individuals they are! ← final
paragraph
restates
opinion

Go to page 71 in the **Practice** the Strategy **Notebook!**

Revising

Elaborate
Add appropriate and convincing facts or reasons to support my opinion.

" I know from the **Rubric** that I need to think of reasons and facts that will convince my audience to agree with me. I can't just try to overpower them with a load of facts. I have to choose facts they care about.

"I took a close look at the paragraph below and decided that one fact had to go. (It was boring!) Then I added another fact that might help convince my readers not to stereotype people. "

[2nd DRAFT]

It's really a dumb mistake to stereotype Californians. ~~In the 1990 census, California had more than 29 million residents.~~ More than half of Californians were born someplace else, and he moved there. Between 1970 and 1990, the poplulation of California grew by 50 percent. Many of these new residents came from the northeastern and southern states. California also has more imigrants from other countries than any other state. How could you group all these people together? How could you say they are all the same?

boring fact

added fact to convince audience

Between 1990 and 1999, 233,000 people moved to California from Oregon!

Go to page 74 in the **Practice Notebook!**
the Strategy

Persuasive Writing • Persuasive Essay

Revising

Clarify

Check to see that I have avoided using loaded words.

> I feel strongly about my opinion, and I want to make it clear. Yet when I read my persuasive essay to myself, I realized that I might be using loaded words to sway readers unfairly. I replaced those words with more objective words. Now my essay seems more reasonable than emotional. You can see how it helped in this paragraph.

READ TO MYSELF

Loaded Word

A **loaded word** has an emotional meaning. It can be a positive meaning or a negative one. For example, *shack* is a negatively loaded word for *house*. *Mansion* is a positively loaded word. Loaded words can influence a reader's thinking unfairly.

replaced loaded word

deleted loaded word

[3rd DRAFT]

Stereotyping is wrong. It's a kind of prejudice. Some ~~ignorant~~

people use stereotypes to ~~jump to~~ make decisions. They decide whether

they like people because of the group they belong to. They don't

~~bother~~ take the time to get to know him. It's like being prejudiced against people

because of the ~~shabby~~ kind of clothes they wear or the ~~strange~~ language

she speaks. You could miss meeting good friends if you make deci-

sions based on stereotypes.

replaced loaded words

deleted loaded word

Go to page 76 in the **Practice Notebook!** the Strategy

Editing

Proofread

Check to see that each pronoun has a clear antecedent and that the pronoun and antecedent agree.

> I've finally reached my fourth draft! Now I have to fix my mistakes in spelling, grammar, and punctuation. I also need to make sure my pronouns and antecedents match and that each pronoun has a clear antecedent. If I'm not careful with my pronouns, my audience will wonder who or what I'm talking about.
>
> "I like this part of the revision. It's like I'm panning for gold nuggets, only I'm looking for errors instead!"

Pronouns and Antecedents

The **antecedent** for a **pronoun** should be clear. It should be easy to tell which word the pronoun is replacing. A pronoun must also be the same number and gender as its antecedent.

Unclear antecedent:
Californians welcome visitors; **they** enjoy the warm climate. (It's unclear whether *they* refers to *Californians* or *visitors*.)

Clear antecedent:
Visitors are welcome in California; **they** enjoy the warm climate. (*They* clearly refers to *visitors*.)

Pronouns that agree:
My mother is from California. **She** taught me not to judge others unfairly. (*She* is singular and refers to a female, so it agrees with its antecedent, *mother*.)

Keith and Joy are from California. **They** love it there. (*They* is plural because it refers to two antecedents, *Keith* and *Joy*.)

Extra Practice
See **Pronouns and Antecedents** (pages CS 12–CS 13) in the back of this book.

" Here's most of my fourth draft, so you can see the kinds of errors I corrected. "

[4th DRAFT]

Don't Stereotype by State!
by Anthony

(sp)
Do you think all Californians pay ~~way~~ too much attention to how

they look? Do you think they all follow the latest fads, no matter

                    temporary?   group
how ~~stupid?~~ When we ~~lump~~ people together for some reason, we

are stereotyping them. In this case, we are forming an opinion

about them based on where they live. That's wrong! The people who

live in California are as different from each other as the people

                                            Californians!   ← unclear
who live in every state. We must stop stereotyping ~~them!~~   antecedent

matches Stereotyping is wrong. It's a kind of prejudice. Some people use
antecedent

stereotypes to make decisions. They decide whether they like peo-

                            those people
ple because of the group ~~they~~ belong to. They don't take the time

                    them
to get to know ~~him.~~ It's like being prejudiced against people

because of the kind of clothes they wear or the language

they speak
~~she speaks.~~ You could miss meeting good friends if you make deci-

sions based on stereotypes.

            unwise
It's really ~~a dumb mistake~~ to stereotype Californians. More than   matches
                                                they ←   antecedent
half of Californians were born someplace else. Then ~~he~~ moved to

California.

Go to page 77 in the **Practice the Strategy Notebook!**

Publishing

Share

Publish my persuasive essay on a class bulletin board.

Writer: Anthony

Assignment: persuasive essay

Topic: stereotyping

Audience: classmates

Method of Publication: "What I Think" bulletin board

Reason for Choice: The class can easily read my persuasive essay.

  " The class bulletin board gives students a chance to express their ideas on all sorts of topics. It's a good way for us to share our opinions.

  "Here are the steps I followed to get my essay ready to display on the bulletin board. After all the essays were posted, it was interesting to read everyone else's essays. **"**

1. First, I checked my essay one more time for mistakes.

2. Next, I wrote "by Anthony" under the title.

3. I made a clean copy of my essay.

4. I posted my essay on the "What I Think" bulletin board.

Don't Stereotype by State!

by Anthony

Do you think all Californians pay too much attention to how they look? Do you think they all follow the latest fads, no matter how temporary? When we group people together for some reason, we are stereotyping them. In this case, we are forming an opinion about them based on where they live. That's wrong! The people who live in California are as different from each other as the people who live in every state. We must stop stereotyping Californians!

Stereotyping is wrong. It's a kind of prejudice. Some people use stereotypes to make decisions. They decide whether they like people because of the group those people belong to. They don't take the time to get to know them. It's like being prejudiced against people because of the kind of clothes they wear or the language they speak. You could miss meeting good friends if you make decisions based on stereotypes.

It's really unwise to stereotype Californians. More than half of Californians were born someplace else. Then they moved to California. Between 1970 and 1990, the population of California grew by 50 percent. Many of these new residents came from the northeastern and southern states. Between 1990 and 1999, 233,000 people moved to California from Oregon! California also has more immigrants from other countries than any other state. How could you group all these people together? How could you say they are all the same?

There is no typical Californian. One in four Californians is Hispanic. In the 1990 census, nearly 5 million Californians said they had German ancestors. Another 3.5 million Californians had Irish ancestors.

Californians have different backgrounds, customs, likes, and dislikes. They're just like people everywhere. Sure, a few pay too much attention to how they look. A few people in our state do, too. Let's treat Californians like the individuals they are!

USING the Rubric for Assessment

Go to page 78 in the **Practice** the Strategy **Notebook!** Use that rubric to assess Anthony's paper. Try using the rubric to assess your own writing.

your own
PERSUASIVE
writing

Responding to Literature

Put the strategies you practiced in this unit to work to write your own book review, persuasive essay, or both! You can:

- develop the writing you did in the Your Own Writing pages of the *Practice the Strategy Notebook*;

- pick an idea below and write something new;

- choose another idea of your own.

Be sure to follow the steps in the writing process. Use the rubrics in this unit to assess your writing.

Book Review

- of a fiction and nonfiction book about the same topic
- of two fiction books illustrated by the same person or people
- of two books by your favorite author

Persuasive Essay

- about a book made into a movie
- about a book that contains strong opinions
- about a book about famous people or inventions

portfolio

School–Home Connection

Keep a writing portfolio. Think about adding the activities from the *Practice the Strategy Notebook* to your writing portfolio. You may want to take your portfolio home to share.

DESCRIPTIVE

writing

describes something to the reader.

1

Descriptive Essay

2

Observation Report

DESCRIPTIVE writing

Descriptive Essay

In this chapter, you will work with one kind of descriptive writing: a **descriptive essay**.

A **descriptive essay** gives a clear, detailed picture of a person, place, thing, or event.

On the next page are a photograph and a descriptive essay about the photograph. Read the questions below. Then look at the photograph and read the essay, keeping the questions in mind.

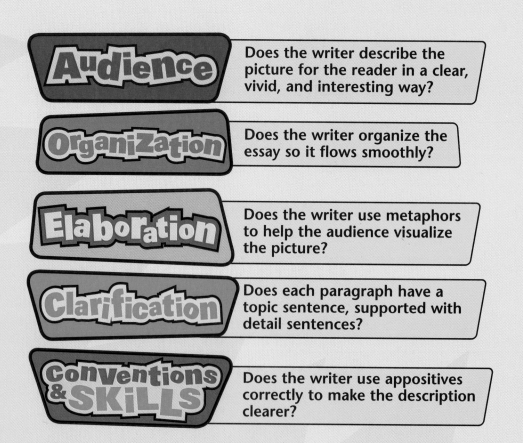

Audience
Does the writer describe the picture for the reader in a clear, vivid, and interesting way?

Organization
Does the writer organize the essay so it flows smoothly?

Elaboration
Does the writer use metaphors to help the audience visualize the picture?

Clarification
Does each paragraph have a topic sentence, supported with detail sentences?

Conventions & Skills
Does the writer use appositives correctly to make the description clearer?

A Striking Image

by Anna Yuishmal

I was leisurely thumbing through a book about weather recently when I was suddenly struck by lightning —in a photograph. Filling the page was a lightning storm, a monstrous fire in the sky. Against an inky black sky, mounds of angry clouds piled on top of each other. A charred, smoky-gray mass smoldered near the bottom of the photo. A raging orange cloud exploded like lava. Looming above was a brilliant yellow cloudburst, singed red at its edges. The lightning bolts were a tangle of glowing white wires that sliced the night into jagged pieces.

Lightning is a split-second show, a glimpse of nature's awesome energy. Zing! Steely fingers reach out to snatch a piece of the sky. Poof! They are gone. The photographer captured the brief moment. As the lightning flashed, the shutter snapped.

The image reminded me of what comes after a lightning strike. The metallic odor of burnt oxygen, or ozone, follows the flash. Then comes thunder, a distant rolling rumble or a sudden echoing boom. To me, thunder is the delicious dessert after the lightning.

As I closed the book, I could still feel the high-voltage force of the fleeting event caught in the photo. A shiver like a lightning bolt ran down my spine and stayed there.

Using a Rubric

To use a rubric, you assign 1, 2, 3, or 4 points to tell how well the author handled certain writing tasks.

Remember the questions you read on page 140? Those questions were used to make this rubric.

> Hi! My name is Blue Star. How did you like the descriptive essay on page 141? We can learn about descriptive writing by evaluating that essay. We'll use this rubric. First, let's read these questions and the information for each one. Then we'll study the essay. Later, I'm going to write my own descriptive essay. You will probably want to write one, too. Okay, let's get to work.

Audience

Does the writer describe the picture for the reader in a clear, vivid, and interesting way?

Organization

Does the writer organize the essay so it flows smoothly?

Elaboration

Does the writer use metaphors to help the audience visualize the picture?

Clarification

Does each paragraph have a topic sentence, supported with detail sentences?

Conventions & Skills

Does the writer use appositives correctly to make the description clearer?

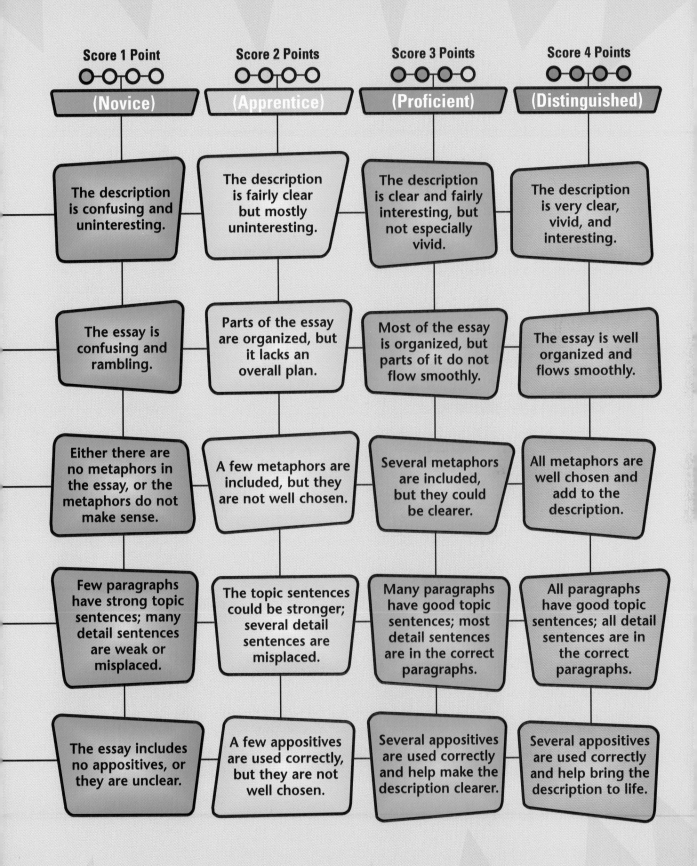

Score 1 Point
(Novice)

Score 2 Points
(Apprentice)

Score 3 Points
(Proficient)

Score 4 Points
(Distinguished)

The description is confusing and uninteresting.

The description is fairly clear but mostly uninteresting.

The description is clear and fairly interesting, but not especially vivid.

The description is very clear, vivid, and interesting.

The essay is confusing and rambling.

Parts of the essay are organized, but it lacks an overall plan.

Most of the essay is organized, but parts of it do not flow smoothly.

The essay is well organized and flows smoothly.

Either there are no metaphors in the essay, or the metaphors do not make sense.

A few metaphors are included, but they are not well chosen.

Several metaphors are included, but they could be clearer.

All metaphors are well chosen and add to the description.

Few paragraphs have strong topic sentences; many detail sentences are weak or misplaced.

The topic sentences could be stronger; several detail sentences are misplaced.

Many paragraphs have good topic sentences; most detail sentences are in the correct paragraphs.

All paragraphs have good topic sentences; all detail sentences are in the correct paragraphs.

The essay includes no appositives, or they are unclear.

A few appositives are used correctly, but they are not well chosen.

Several appositives are used correctly and help make the description clearer.

Several appositives are used correctly and help bring the description to life.

Using a Rubric
to Study the Model

Discuss each question on the rubric with your classmates. Find words and sentences in Anna Yuishmal's descriptive essay that help you answer each question. Decide how many points to give the essay in each category.

Audience

Does the writer describe the picture for the reader in a clear, vivid, and interesting way?

> The writer grabbed my attention with her very first sentence. She says she was struck by lightning! I imagined her being struck while she was looking at the book. Right away, she explains what she means, but she has already made me want to keep reading.

I was leisurely thumbing through a book about weather recently when I was suddenly struck by lightning—in a photograph.

> Then she goes on to describe the photograph with vivid details. You can sense her enthusiasm about this picture.

Does the writer organize the essay so it flows smoothly?

"The first thing you usually want to know is how something looks, so the writer begins by describing the appearance of the storm."

Filling the page was a lightning storm, a monstrous fire in the sky. Against an inky black sky, mounds of angry clouds piled on top of each other. A charred, smoky-gray mass smoldered near the bottom of the photo. A raging orange cloud exploded like lava. Looming above was a brilliant yellow cloudburst, singed red at its edges. The lightning bolts were a tangle of glowing white wires that sliced the night into jagged pieces.

"Then the writer describes how the lightning smells, how it sounds, and how she feels after she closes the book. It's a logical order that flows just right."

Does the writer use metaphors to help the audience visualize the picture?

"The essay is loaded with metaphors. By using metaphors, the writer compares two unlike things to help us 'see' what is in the photograph. One metaphor compares thunder to dessert because thunder comes after lightning, which is like dessert coming after the main course."

The image reminded me of what comes after a lightning strike. The metallic odor of burnt oxygen, or ozone, follows the flash. Then comes thunder, a distant rolling rumble or a sudden echoing boom. To me, thunder is the delicious dessert after the lightning.

Clarification

Does each paragraph have a topic sentence, supported with detail sentences?

" In every paragraph, the writer has a strong topic sentence that tells you what the paragraph is about. For example, you know from the first sentence in this paragraph that it's about the speed of the lightning. The other sentences provide more details about this speed. "

Lightning is a split-second show, a glimpse of nature's awesome energy. Zing! Steely fingers reach out to snatch a piece of the sky. Poof! They are gone. The photographer captured the brief moment. As the lightning flashed, the shutter snapped.

Conventions & SKILLS

Does the writer use appositives correctly to make the description clearer?

" She does! She uses appositives to add more information about the nouns in her sentences. In the sentence below, for example, **ozone** is an appositive that provides more information about the burnt oxygen. She also punctuates appositives correctly by setting them off with commas. "

The metallic odor of burnt oxygen, or ozone, follows the flash.

" **Now it's my turn to write!**

I'm ready to write my own descriptive essay. I already have some ideas. You can come along and watch how I do it. I'm going to use what I learned from the model and the rubric. "

Blue Star

Writer of a
Descriptive Essay

Name:	Blue Star
Home:	Ohio
Volunteer Work:	at the animal shelter twice a week
Recent Accomplishment:	Blue Star's photographs of animals at the shelter hang on the wall there.
Assignment:	descriptive essay

Prewriting

Gather

Choose a picture and take notes about the sensory details in it.

" While I was looking for a picture for our assignment to write a descriptive essay, I found this photograph of a cat and a fish. It was in a magazine ad, and I couldn't stop looking at it. "

Descriptive Writing · Descriptive Essay

> I took these notes on the sensory details in the photograph so I could use them in my essay. I have to use my imagination for the feel, sound, taste, and smell of things in the picture. Actually, I didn't take any notes on smells or tastes. I don't think there are any—unless the cat catches the fish!

Sensory Detail

A **sensory detail** is a descriptive word or phrase that relates to one of the five senses (see, feel, smell, taste, hear). For example, these words give sensory details about a rose: *ruby* (see), *silken* (feel), *fragrant* (smell).

My Notes on the Picture of the Cat and Fish

- **see:** cat looking into fishbowl; looks like cat's face is inside bowl; cat's ears – small pink shark fins; eyes – big baby-blue and black marbles in pink ovals; nose – pale pink; whiskers – white; goldfish – on cat's nose, plump, shiny yellow with bright orange at front, black ink dot for eye, 2 tiny bubbles from open mouth; bowl – open on top, curved edges, water line below cat's ears, white gravel

- **feel:** cat's nose – velvety; ears – fluffy inside; whiskers – sharp; fish's tail – gawzy, delicate

- **hear:** cat saying, "Mmmm"; fish saying, "Oh! oh!"

Go to page 80 in the **Practice** the Strategy **Notebook!**

Prewriting

Organize
Use my notes to make a spider map.

❝ The **Rubric** stresses that my essay should be organized and flow smoothly. My notes are organized by senses, but I see that most of my details are in the 'see' category. I need to break my notes into more categories.

"A spider map can help me better organize my notes. I can make each leg a different category of details, like what you can see of the cat in the photograph, what you can see of the fish, and so on.

"When I get my notes organized into several categories, I will be able to write my essay so it flows smoothly without jumping around. ❞

Spider Map

A **spider map** organizes information about a topic. The topic is written in the center circle. Each leg is one category of details.

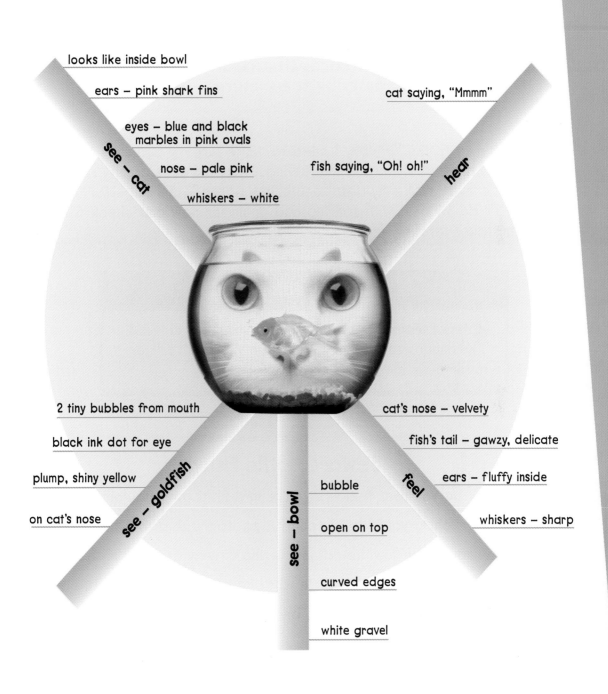

looks like inside bowl

ears – pink shark fins

cat saying, "Mmmm"

eyes – blue and black
marbles in pink ovals

see – cat

nose – pale pink

fish saying, "Oh! oh!"

hear

whiskers – white

2 tiny bubbles from mouth

cat's nose – velvety

black ink dot for eye

fish's tail – gawzy, delicate

plump, shiny yellow

see – goldfish

bubble

ears – fluffy inside

feel

on cat's nose

see – bowl

whiskers – sharp

open on top

curved edges

white gravel

Go to page 82 in the Practice the Strategy Notebook!

Drafting

Write
Draft my essay. Include detail sentences that clearly and vividly describe the picture.

"According to the **Rubric**, I need to make sure my audience thinks my essay is clear, vivid, and interesting. My classmates are my audience. I'll try to make my detail sentences pop off the page for them! I'll do my best with spelling and grammar now and check for any mistakes later."

Detail Sentence

A **detail sentence** supports the paragraph's main idea. The detail sentences in a paragraph should all relate to the main idea.

[1st DRAFT]

detail sentence

Beware, Little Fishy!

Do you ever feel like you're in a fishbowl and someone is watching you? Well, I found a photograph about that feeling. ~~Inside~~ A white cat is peering intently at a goldfish in a bowl. The water distorts what you see. It looks like the cat's face is INSIDE the bowl, and the cat's face looks HUGE!

detail sentences ⎯

detail sentences

The cat's staring eyes, big blue marbles with black centers, are set in pink ovals. Its ears are like pink shark fins, with tuffs of white fluff inside. ~~The water~~ ᵛThe ears are above the water line, so they aren't distorted. They are much smaller than the eyes and closer together. The fish's eye glances backward nervously. White whiskers ~~grow~~ ᵛsprowt from the cat's furry cheeks. Its nose is pale pink.

detail sentences

The goldfish is ~~really~~ ᵛparticarly appealing. Its plump little body is shiny yellow, with a bright orange face and shoulders. Its gawzy, delicate tail casts a shadow on the cat's cheek.

When you look at the picture, you can imagine what the cat and the fish are thinking and saying. ~~You can~~ ᵛThe cat, a silent and sly hunter is thinking about the juicey orange goldfish. The cat murmurs, "Mmmm," and the fish replies, "Oh! Oh!" Two tiny bubbles float up. ~~Mostly~~ ᵛNormally the little fish is probably care-free, but it seems to ~~know~~ ᵛsense the possible danger. The curving sides of the bowl ~~make a~~ frame the tense situation. Beware, little fishy! You may feel safe behind your glass wall, but remember this: the bowl is open on top!

detail sentences

Go to page 83 in the Practice the Strategy Notebook!

Revising

Elaborate

Add metaphors to help the reader visualize the picture.

> As I read my first draft, I wondered if my reader would be able to picture the cat in the fishbowl. Then I remembered that the **Rubric** recommends using metaphors to help describe things. I added a metaphor about the fish's tail. I really think it will help my reader picture the tail. I thought of a metaphor for the cat's nose, too, so I added it.

Metaphor

A **metaphor** compares two different things. For example, in "Its ears are the fins of prowling pink sharks," the writer is comparing a cat's ears with shark fins. A metaphor is like a simile, but it does not use the word *like* or *as*.

[2nd DRAFT]

is a waving fan that ← **Added metaphor compares the tail to a fan.**

Its gawzy, delicate tail casts a shadow on the cat's cheek.

---

pale pink a velvety cushion for the goldfish.

Its nose is ~~pale pink~~

Added metaphor compares the nose to a cushion.

---

the Strategy

Go to page 85 in the **Practice Notebook!**

Revising

Clarify

Make sure every paragraph has a topic sentence and all the detail sentences relate to that topic.

READ TO A PARTNER

"My teacher said I'm going to be reading my essay aloud, so I read my second draft to my friend, Naomi. She has a good ear.

"Naomi pointed out that I need a topic sentence in the paragraph below. The paragraph tells how the cat's face is scary but sweet, so I added a topic sentence that says that.

"Naomi also pointed out that one detail sentence in this paragraph is not about the cat's face, so it shouldn't be there. I will move it to my last paragraph, which is about the fish feeling nervous."

Topic Sentence

The **topic sentence** states the main idea of a paragraph. It is often the first sentence in the paragraph, but it may be in the middle or at the end of the paragraph.

[3rd DRAFT]

added topic sentence

detail sentence to be moved

The cat's face is scary but sweet. Its

~~The cat's~~ staring eyes, big blue marbles with black centers, are set in pink ovals. Its ears are the fins of prowling pink sharks, with tuffs of white fluff inside. The ears are above the water line, so they aren't distorted. They are much smaller than the eyes and closer together. The fish's eye an inky black dot glances backward nervously. Spears of white whiskers sprowt from the cat's furry cheeks. Its pale pink nose is a velvety cushion for the goldfish.

Go to page 86 in the **Practice** the Strategy **Notebook!**

Editing

Proofread

Check to see that I have used appositives correctly.

“Wow, I'm almost done! I need to check my draft for mistakes in spelling, capitalization, and punctuation.

“I have to check another skill, too: using appositives correctly. Sometimes I forget the commas, but I'm getting better with practice.”

Appositives

An **appositive** is a word or phrase that follows a noun and helps to identify or describe the noun. An appositive is usually separated from the rest of the sentence by commas.

Examples:

The goldfish, **a popular aquarium fish,** prefers cold water.

White fur in cats is caused by absence of pigment, or **coloration**.

Extra Practice

See **Appositives** (pages CS 14–CS 15) in the back of this book.

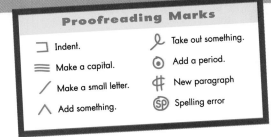

Proofreading Marks

⌐ Indent.

𝓮 Take out something.

≡ Make a capital.

⊙ Add a period.

/ Make a small letter.

New paragraph

∧ Add something.

(SP) Spelling error

66 Here's part of my fourth draft, so you can see the kinds of errors I corrected. 99

[4th DRAFT]

added comma to set off appositive

Shimmering in the center of the glass bubble, the goldfish is (SP) ul particarly appealing. Its plump little body is shiny yellow, with a bright orange face and shoulders. Its (SP) gawzy, delicate tail is a waving fan that casts a shadow on the cat's cheek.

When you look at the picture, you can imagine what the cat and the fish might be thinking and saying. The cat, a silent and sly hunter, is thinking about the (SP) juicey orange goldfish. The cat murmurs, "Mmmm," and the fish replies, "Oh! Oh!" Two tiny bubbles float up. # Normally carefree, the goldfish seems to sense the possible danger. Its eye, an inky black dot, glances backward nervously. The curving sides of the bowl frame the tense situation. Beware, little fishy! You may feel safe behind your glass wall, but remember this: the bowl is open on top!

added commas to set off appositive

the Strategy
Go to page 87 in the **Practice** ∧ **Notebook!**

Publishing

Share

Read my essay to my classmates. Ask them to draw their own pictures based on my essay. Discuss how closely their pictures match my description.

Writer: Blue Star

Assignment: descriptive essay

Topic: picture of a cat and a fish

Audience: classmates

Method of Publication: oral reading, followed by a comparison with the picture

Reason for Choice: to test our powers of description

"Our class likes to do art projects and discuss them. This was a good way to explore how written descriptions can help us understand pictures. It also helps us improve our abilities to observe, describe, and even listen! Here's how I prepared for my oral reading."

1. I checked my descriptive essay one more time for mistakes.

2. Then I made a clean copy of my essay and added my name as author.

3. Before my reading, I gave my classmates white paper and colored markers.

4. Then I read my essay aloud and asked my classmates to make their own drawings based on my description.

5. I showed my classmates my picture, and we discussed how closely my description matched the picture.

Beware, Little Fishy!

by Blue Star

Do you ever feel like you're in a fishbowl and someone is watching you? Well, I found a photograph about that feeling. A white cat is peering intently at a goldfish in a bowl. The water distorts what you see, so it looks like the cat's face is INSIDE the bowl, and it's HUGE!

The cat's face is scary but sweet. Its staring eyes, big blue marbles with black centers, are set in pink ovals. Its ears are the fins of prowling pink sharks, with tufts of white fluff inside. The ears are above the water line, so they aren't distorted. They are much smaller than the eyes and set closer together. Spears of white whiskers sprout from the cat's furry cheeks. Its pale pink nose is a velvety cushion for the goldfish.

Shimmering in the center of the glass bubble, the goldfish is particularly appealing. Its plump little body is shiny yellow, with a bright orange face and shoulders. Its gauzy, delicate tail is a waving fan that casts a shadow on the cat's cheek.

When you look at the picture, you can imagine what the cat and the fish might be thinking and saying. The cat, a silent and sly hunter, is thinking about the juicy orange goldfish. The cat murmurs, "Mmmm," and the fish replies, "Oh! Oh!" Two tiny bubbles float up.

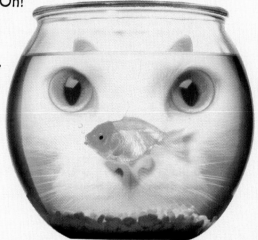

Normally carefree, the goldfish seems to sense the possible danger. Its eye, an inky black dot, glances backward nervously. The curving sides of the bowl frame the tense situation. Beware, little fishy! You may feel safe behind your glass wall, but remember this: the bowl is open on top!

USING the Rubric for Assessment

Go to pages 88–89 in the **Practice Notebook!** Use that rubric to assess Blue Star's essay. Try using the rubric to assess your own writing.

the Strategy

DESCRIPTIVE writing

Observation Report

In this chapter, you will work with one kind of descriptive writing: an **observation report**.

An **observation report** describes in detail an object, person, event, or process. This report is similar to an eyewitness account, but in an observation report, the emphasis is more on descriptive details than on a narration of events.

On the next page is an observation report that is based on a science experiment. Read these questions. Then read the observation report, keeping these questions in mind.

Audience — Does the writer describe the experiment clearly so the reader can visualize each step?

Organization — Does the writer explain the steps in the order they were completed?

Elaboration — Does the writer include diagrams or charts to complete the description?

Clarification — Does the writer use time-order words to clarify the order of events?

Conventions & Skills — Does the writer use apostrophes correctly in possessive nouns and contractions?

GROWING PAINTBRUSH MOLD

by Mark Volk

Penicillium notatum, a green mold that grows on cheese, bread, and fruit, is the source of penicillin, an antibiotic. I already knew that mold grows better in a moist environment. I wondered how temperature affects this mold's growth. My prediction was that the mold would grow better in a warm environment than in a cold environment.

PROCEDURE

Step 1: First, I rubbed two lemons on the floor to roughen up their skin. Then I left them on the kitchen table overnight. This way, penicillin mold spores, which are in soil and air, would be more likely to stick to the fruit.

Step 2: The next day, I put one of the lemons and one moist cotton ball in a paper bag and closed the bag loosely. I put the bag in the refrigerator. Then I repeated this process with the other lemon and put that paper bag in a warm corner of the kitchen.

Step 3: For the next two weeks, I checked the lemons every day, took notes in my Observation Log, and made several color sketches.

Step 4: At the end of the two weeks, one lemon was covered with green mold. I scraped a little of this mold into a drop of water on a microscope slide and looked at it. I didn't get too close to the mold or breathe in any of it. Then I sketched the slide for my Observation Log.

OBSERVATIONS

During the whole experiment, the lemon in the refrigerator didn't change much. By the end of the experiment, it was a little drier but still firm and bright yellow. However, on the third day the lemon in the warm corner began to show spots of green powder. By the end of the two weeks, it had turned into a spongy, aqua-colored fuzz ball. It also had a strong smell because it had started to rot.

Under the microscope, the mold looked like a cluster of stems with feathery ends—something like a paintbrush. That makes sense because penicillin is named for the Latin word *penicillus,* which means "paintbrush."

CONCLUSION

Penicillin grew on the lemon kept in warmth, but not on the one in the refrigerator. A warm environment is better than a cold one for growing penicillin mold.

Using a Rubric

To use a rubric, you assign 1, 2, 3, or 4 points to describe how well the author handled certain writing tasks. Remember the questions you read on page 160? Those questions were used to make this rubric.

"Hey, how's it going? I'm Zachary. Did you read the observation report on page 161? I'm learning how to write a report like that one to describe my science experiments. You can, too. We can use this rubric to help us. Start by reading the questions. Then read the information for each question. After that, we're ready to evaluate this report."

Audience

Does the writer describe the experiment clearly so the reader can visualize each step?

Organization

Does the writer explain the steps in the order they were completed?

Elaboration

Does the writer include diagrams or charts to complete the description?

Clarification

Does the writer use time-order words to clarify the order of events?

Conventions & Skills

Does the writer use apostrophes correctly in possessive nouns and contractions?

Score 1 Point	Score 2 Points	Score 3 Points	Score 4 Points
(Novice)	**(Apprentice)**	**(Proficient)**	**(Distinguished)**
The report does not describe the steps in the procedure.	The report mentions most of the steps but does not describe them clearly.	The report describes most steps clearly.	The report describes all steps clearly so the reader can easily understand what was done.
The steps are mentioned in random order.	Some steps are described in time-order, but others are out of order.	Most steps are described in time-order, but a few are out of order.	All steps are described in the order they were completed.
No diagrams or charts are included.	A diagram or chart is included, but its purpose is not clear.	A diagram or chart is included, but its purpose could be clearer.	One or more diagrams or charts are included and help complete the description of the experiment.
Few time-order words are used, and they do not make the order of events clearer.	A few time-order words are used effectively.	Several time-order words are used effectively.	Many time-order words make the order of events clear.
Few apostrophes are used correctly in possessive nouns or contractions.	Some apostrophes are used correctly.	Most apostrophes are used correctly.	All apostrophes are used correctly.

Descriptive Writing • Observation Report

Using a

Rubric

to Study the Model

Discuss each question on the rubric with your classmates. Find words and sentences in the report that help you answer each one and evaluate the report.

Audience

Does the writer describe the experiment clearly so the reader can visualize each step?

"The writer uses headings to make it easy to see how the report is organized. Then in each step, he tells what he did and, for some steps, why he did it. Here are his first two steps. They are so clear that I could follow them and do the same experiment!"

PROCEDURE

Step 1: First, I rubbed two lemons on the floor to roughen up their skin. Then I left them on the kitchen table overnight. This way, penicillin mold spores, which are in soil and air, would be more likely to stick to the fruit.

Step 2: The next day, I put one of the lemons and one moist cotton ball in a paper bag and closed the bag loosely. I put the bag in the refrigerator. Then I repeated this process with the other lemon and put that paper bag in a warm corner of the kitchen.

Does the writer explain the steps in the order they were completed?

> The writer numbers each step and describes them in order. You know exactly what he did first, second, and so on. Here are his last two steps.

Step 3: For the next two weeks, I checked the lemons every day, took notes in my Observation Log, and made several color sketches.

Step 4: At the end of the two weeks, one lemon was covered with green mold. I scraped a little of the mold into a drop of water on a microscope slide and looked at it. I didn't get too close to the mold or breathe in any of it. Then I sketched the slide for my Observation Log.

Does the writer include diagrams or charts to complete the description?

> I like the drawing of the penicillin mold that he included. I can see what this mold looks like under a microscope— and why its name means 'paintbrush.' I would also like to see the writer's Observation Log that he mentioned in Step 3. I think that would have been interesting, too.

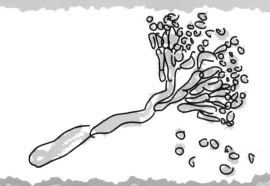

Clarification

Does the writer use time-order words to clarify the order of events?

❝ The report uses time-order words and phrases to let the reader know when each step or each change occurs. **During the whole experiment, By the end of the experiment, on the third day,** and other phrases tell you exactly when he observed changes—or no changes. ❞

OBSERVATIONS

During the whole experiment, the lemon in the refrigerator didn't change much. By the end of the experiment, it was a little drier but still firm and bright yellow. However, on the third day the lemon in the warm corner began to show spots of green powder. By the end of the two weeks, it had turned into a spongy, aqua-colored fuzz ball. It also had a strong smell because it had started to rot.

Does the writer use apostrophes correctly in possessive nouns and contractions?

❝ This writer always uses apostrophes correctly. You can see one of his contractions in the first sentence in the example above—**didn't**. The sentence below includes one of his possessive nouns—**mold's**—with the apostrophe placed correctly, of course. ❞

I wondered how temperature affects this mold's growth.

❝ Now it's my turn to write!

I'm going to write an observation report that shows how much I learned from the model and the rubric. You can follow along to see how I do it! ❞

Zachary

Writer of an Observation Report

Name: Zachary

Home: Arkansas

Hobbies: slot car racing, collecting model cars

Favorite Model: 1957 Plymouth Fury 10-inch diecast metal model

Favorite Book: *Maniac Magee* by Jerry Spinelli

Assignment: observation report

Prewriting

Gather Observe and take notes.

❝Our teacher asked us to work with partners for this assignment. One partner will do an experiment, and the other one will write an observation report on the experiment.

"I was surprised to find out that Lisa, my partner, is interested in cars and speed, just like me. We found a book in the library that has experiments in speed. One experiment shows how gravity affects acceleration (how fast an object starts to move). In this experiment, different numbers of weights were attached to a model car with a long string. Then the weights were dropped over the side of a table. Gravity pulled on the weights, and the weights pulled the car across the table at different rates of acceleration. A cardboard bumper stopped the car.

"We decided that Lisa would do the experiment, and I would write the report.❞

My Notes on the Acceleration Experiment

- **Our question:** How would attaching more weights to a car affect its acceleration?
- **Our prediction:** Each additional weight would increase the car's acceleration.
- **What we did:** attached paper clip hook to car with string; put one weight (washer) on hook and hung it over edge; held car 2.5 ft from edge; let car go and started timing with stopwatch; stopped timing when car hit cardboard bumper; recorded time in log; averaged time over 3 runs; repeated with more weights.
- **The results (averages):** 1 weight: car hit bumper in 2.6 seconds; 2 weights: car hit in 1.8 seconds; 3 weights: 1.4 seconds; 4 weights: 1.1 seconds; 5 weights: .7 seconds
- **Conclusion:** Our prediction is correct. More weights mean a faster acceleration rate.

Go to page 90 in the Practice the Strategy Notebook!

Descriptive Writing • Observation Report

Prewriting

Organize

Use my notes to make a sequence chain of the steps in the experiment.

> **66** According to the **Rubric**, I need to explain the steps in our experiment in the order we did them. That way, readers can understand what we did and maybe even do the same experiment themselves. A sequence chain is a good way to put the steps in order. **99**

Sequence Chain

A **sequence chain** shows steps or events in the order they happen.

Step 1: To set up the experiment, we
  a) made a paper clip into a hook.
  b) used tape to mark a starting line 2.5 ft from the edge of a table.
  c) taped a cardboard bumper to the edge of the table to stop the car; made a hole at the bottom of the bumper for the string.
  d) cut 2.5 ft of string; tied one end to the car's axel and the other end to the hook.
  e) pushed the hook through the hole in the bumper.

Step 2: Lisa put one weight on the hook.

Step 3: Next, she held the weight over the edge of the table.

Step 4: With her other hand, she put the car at the starting line.

Step 5: She let the weight fall, and I started the stopwatch.

Step 6: I stopped timing when the car hit the bumper. I recorded the time.

Step 7: We repeated Steps 2–6 two more times. Then we averaged the times.

Step 8: We repeated Steps 2–7 with 2, 3, 4, and 5 weights. We recorded and averaged the times.

Go to page 92 in the **Practice the Strategy Notebook!**

Drafting

Write

Draft my report. Include a short introduction, a description of the steps, observations, and conclusions.

"Now it's time to write my report. My parents, my classmates, and their parents are going to read it. The **Rubric** says that I need to describe the experiment clearly so they can visualize each step. My sequence chain will help make sure that I don't leave out any steps. I'll also add an introduction, observations, and my conclusion.

"I'll use headings to show the parts of the report, like the model report did. They will make my report easier to read.

"As for spelling and grammar, I will do my best now and check for mistakes later. Right now, I need to get my first draft on paper. You can read part of my draft. I still have to write the Observations and Conclusions sections."

[1st DRAFT]

How Gravity Affects Acceleration

introduction

Gravity is one of Earths forces. It keeps ~~stuff~~ everything from floating off into space. Lisa and I did an experiment with a model car to see how gravity affects aceleration—how fast the car starts to move. We decided to attach a weight to one end of a string, tie the other end to the car, and drop the weight over the ege of a table. As gravity pulled the weight down, the weight would pull the car across the table. Lisa and I predickted that as we added more weights, the car would accelerate faster.

PROCEDURE

Step 1: Lisa twisted a paper clip into a hook. She used tape to mark a starting line on a table 2.5 ft from the edge. She taped a piece of cardboard to the edge of the table. This bumper would stop the car from falling off the table. She made a small opening at the bottom of the bumper for the string to slide through. I cut 2.5 ft of string. Lisa tied one end to the cars axel and the other end to the hook. She pushed the hook through the opening in the bumper.

Step 2: Lisa slipped one weight on the hook.

Step 3: Then she held the weight over the edge of the table.

Step 4: She put the car at the starting line and held it their. Thats when we figured out that I would have to work the stopwatch. Lisa already had her hands full!

Step 5: Lisa let the weight fall, and I started the stopwatch.

Step 6: I stopped the stopwatch when the car hit the bumper. I had to practice this several times. That car moved fast!

Step 7: Lisa and I timed the car with one ~~wait~~ weight on it two more times. Then I added the times and divided by 3 to get the average. I wrote that in our Obseration Log.

Step 8: Then we repeated the hole process with 2, 3, 4, and 5 weights hanging on the hook. We did each number of weights 3 times and averaged the speed.

OBSERVATIONS (to be completed)

CONCLUSION (to be completed)

Go to page 94 in the **Practice** the Strategy **Notebook!**

Revising

Elaborate
Add diagrams or charts to complete the description.

READ TO A PARTNER

" After I read my report to Lisa, she wondered if our classmates would understand what we had done. It sounded kind of confusing. Then I remembered what the **Rubric** said about adding diagrams or charts. That would help! Then our readers could see what we had done.

"I already had filled in our Observation Log, so I added that to my Observations section. I also drew a diagram to show how we set up the experiment. "

[2nd DRAFT]

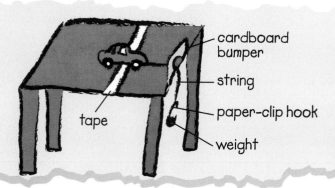

- cardboard bumper
- string
- paper-clip hook
- weight
- tape

	Observation Log			
	Time in Seconds to Reach Tables Edge			
Number of Weights	**Run #1**	**Run #2**	**Run #3**	**Average**
1	2.7	2.6	2.6	2.6
2	1.7	1.9	1.8	1.8
3	1.4	1.2	1.6	1.4
4	1.2	1.1	1.0	1.1
5	.8	.5	.9	.7

Go to page 96 in the **Practice the Strategy Notebook!**

Revising

Clarify — Add time-order words where they are needed.

" Writing the report in steps helped show the order in which Lisa and I did things. However, I knew I could add more time-order words, especially in the part where I explained how we set up the experiment. Lisa agreed. "

Time-Order Words

Time-order words help show when different steps or events take place. They include words such as *after, during, first, second, third, until, meanwhile, next, soon, later, finally, then,* and *as soon as.*

[3rd DRAFT]

time-order words

Step 1: To begin setting up the experiment, Lisa twisted a paper clip into a hook. Next, She used tape to mark a starting line on a table. I helped her measure 2.5 ft from the edge. Then She taped a piece of cardboard to the edge of the table. This bumper would stop the car from falling off the table. She remembered to make a small opening at the bottom of the bumper for the string to slide through. Meanwhile, I cut 2.5 ft of string. Lisa tied one end to the car's axel and the other end to the hook. To finish setting up, She pushed the hook through the opening at the bottom of the bumper.

time-order words

Go to page 98 in the **Practice** the Strategy **Notebook!**

Editing

Proofread

Check to see that I used apostrophes correctly in possessive nouns and contractions.

" My last step is to check for spelling, grammar, and punctuation errors. The **Rubric** reminds me to make sure I used apostrophes correctly in possessive nouns and contractions. Now's the time for me to do that. "

Apostrophes

To form the **possessive** of a singular noun, add an apostrophe and *s*.

Example: A driver controls a car**'s** speed with the accelerator.

To form the **possessive** of a plural noun that ends in *s*, just add an apostrophe.

Example: Slot car racers control their cars**'** speed with a special device.

To form the **possessive** of a plural noun that does not end in *s*, add an apostrophe and *s*.

Example: Slot car racing is not just a children**'s** sport.

To form a **contraction,** use an apostrophe to replace dropped letters.

Example: We**'re** here to do some racing!

Extra Practice

See **Apostrophes** (pages CS 16–CS 17) in the back of this book.

Descriptive Writing · Observation Report

"Here's part of my fourth draft, so you can see the kinds of errors I corrected."

OBSERVATIONS   apostrophe in a contraction   [4th DRAFT]

When I looked at our Observation Log, I didn't see a pattern at first, but Lisa pointed it out. As the number of weights increased, the time decreased.

apostrophe to show possession

Observation Log
Time in Seconds to Reach Tables Edge

Number of Weights	Run #1	Run #2	Run #3	Average
1	2.7	2.6	2.6	2.6
2	1.7	1.9	1.8	1.8
3	1.4	1.2	1.6	1.4
4	1.2	1.1	1.0	1.1
5	.8	.5	.9	.7

apostrophe to show possession

CONCLUSION   apostrophe in a contraction

It's clear. The numbers say it all. Adding weights increased gravity's pull on the weights. The more weights we added, the faster the car accelerated across the table. Our prediction was correct.

no apostrophe; plural, not possessive

Go to page 99 in the Practice the Strategy Notebook!

Descriptive Writing · Observation Report

Publishing

Share Display the report on Family Night.

> **Writer:** Zachary
> **Assignment:** observation report
> **Topic:** experiment in acceleration
> **Audience:** classmates and parents
> **Method of Publication:** display my report on Family Night
> **Reason for Choice:** to show how well we describe science experiments

" When you carry out science experiments, you have to observe carefully and record your observations in writing. Our class decided to display our observation reports on science experiments during Family Night because our reports were so good. Here's how Lisa and I got our report ready for display. "

1. We checked the report one more time for mistakes.

2. Then we decided to add both our names as authors because we both contributed to the experiment and the report.

3. I drew a neat, larger copy of the set-up diagram and added it to the final report. We taped the Observation Log in a space we had left in the report.

4. We put the report on posterboard to display on Family Night. We stood the posterboard up behind the model car.

How Gravity Affects Acceleration
by Lisa and Zachary

Gravity is one of Earth's forces. It keeps everything from floating off into space. Lisa and I did an experiment with a model car to see how gravity affects acceleration—how fast the car starts to move. We decided to attach a weight to one end of a string, tie the other end to the car, and drop the weight over the edge of a table. As gravity pulled the weight down, the weight would pull the car across the table. Lisa and I predicted that as we added more weight, the car would accelerate faster.

PROCEDURE

Step 1: To begin setting up the experiment, Lisa twisted a paper clip into a hook. Next, she used tape to mark a starting line on a table. I helped her measure 2.5 feet from the edge of the table. Then she taped a piece of cardboard to the edge of the table. This bumper would stop the car from falling off the table. She remembered to make a small opening at the bottom of the bumper for the string to slide through. Meanwhile, I cut 2.5 feet of string. Lisa tied one end to the car's axle and the other end to the hook. To finish setting up, she pushed the hook through the opening at the bottom of the bumper.

Step 2: Lisa slipped one weight on the hook.

Step 3: Then she held the weight over the edge of the table.

Step 4: She put the car at the starting line and held it there. That's when we figured out that I would have to work the stopwatch. Lisa already had her hands full!

Step 5: Lisa let the weight fall, and I started the stopwatch.

Step 6: I stopped the stopwatch when the car hit the bumper. Actually, I had to practice this several times before I could do it right. That car moved fast!

Step 7: Lisa and I timed the car with one weight on it two more times. Then I added the times and divided by 3 to get the average. I wrote that in our Observation Log.

Step 8: Then we repeated the whole process with 2, 3, 4, and 5 weights hanging on the hook. We did each number of weights 3 times and averaged the speed.

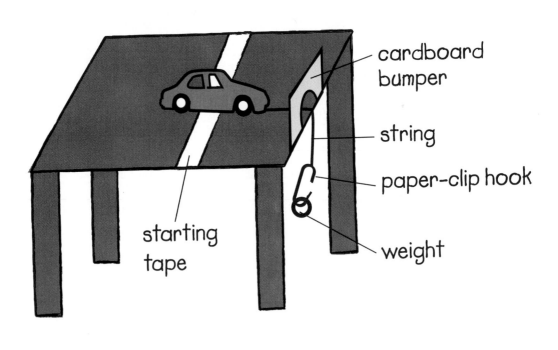

cardboard bumper

string

paper-clip hook

weight

starting tape

OBSERVATIONS

When I looked at our Observation Log, I didn't see a pattern at first, but Lisa pointed it out. As the number of weights increased, the time decreased.

Observation Log
Time in Seconds to Reach Table's Edge

Number of Weights	Run #1	Run #2	Run #3	Average
1	2.7	2.6	2.6	2.6
2	1.7	1.9	1.8	1.8
3	1.4	1.2	1.6	1.4
4	1.2	1.1	1.0	1.1
5	.8	.5	.9	.7

CONCLUSION

It's clear. The numbers say it all. Adding weights increased gravity's pull on the weights. The more weights we added, the faster the car accelerated across the table. Our prediction was correct.

USING the Rubric for Assessment

Go to page 100 in the **Practice Notebook!** the Strategy Use that rubric to assess Zachary and Lisa's paper. Try using the rubric to assess your own writing.

your own

DESCRIPTIVE writing

Art

Put the strategies you practiced in this unit to work to write your own descriptive essay, observation report, or both! You can:

- develop the writing you did in the Your Own Writing pages of the *Practice the Strategy Notebook*;
- pick an idea below and write something new;
- choose another idea of your own.

Be sure to follow the steps in the writing process. Use the rubrics in this unit to assess your writing.

Descriptive Essay
• about a painting of a stormy sea
• about an old photograph of someone in your family or a historical event
• about an illustration created on a computer
• about a sculpture of an animal or person

Observation Report
• on an experiment on how filters affect a camera lens
• on an experiment on how acid rain affects outdoor statues
• on an experiment on the centrifugal force of a pottery wheel

portfolio

School–Home Connection

Keep a writing portfolio. Think about adding the activities from the *Practice the Strategy Notebook* to your writing portfolio. You may want to take your portfolio home to share.

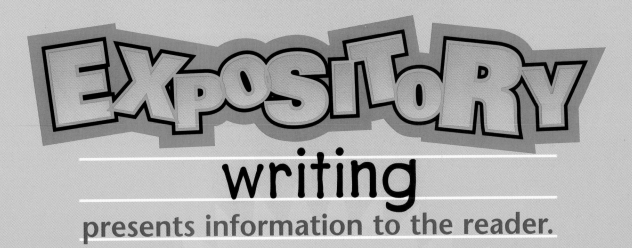

EXPOSITORY writing

presents information to the reader.

1

Cause-and-Effect Report

2

Research Report

EXPOSITORY writing

Cause-and-Effect Report

In this chapter, you will work with one kind of expository writing: a **cause-and-effect report**.

A **cause-and-effect report** might tell how a cause or causes produce certain effects. It might also describe certain effects and trace them back to their causes.

On the next page is a cause-and-effect report. Read these questions. Then read the report, keeping the questions in mind.

 Does the writer grab and hold the audience's attention?

 Does the writer organize the report so it follows a cause-and-effect pattern?

 Does the writer include supporting facts and reasons?

 Does the writer avoid using sentences that are too long and confusing?

 Does the writer use subject and object pronouns correctly, especially *who* and *whom*?

Understanding the Barrier Islands

by Julia Tazzi

The barrier islands are called the "children of the sea." Born after the last ice age, they stretch along the Atlantic coast in long, narrow chains. Some of these chains extend for 100 miles or more. The islands have been around for nearly 18 centuries, but they may not exist forever.

What caused the islands to form? At the end of the ice age, the air warmed and the glaciers melted. The melting ice caused rivers and streams to rise. As they flooded over the beaches, they carried sand and sediment to shallow areas just off the Atlantic coast. Ridges formed there. Then waves deposited more sand on the ridges. The ridges slowly became islands. Ocean currents pushed the sand up and down the islands. That caused them to lengthen into narrow strips.

The barrier islands have broad beaches and dunes on the ocean side. They have mud flats and salt marshes on the mainland side. This low, sandy structure is vulnerable to erosion. However, plants in the dunes, flats, and marshes help stabilize the islands. The plants and the dunes themselves slow the wind. As the wind slows down, it is not strong enough to pick up sand and carry it away. Plant roots also hold the sand in place.

Natural erosion isn't the only danger to these islands. People who enjoy the beach love to vacation on the barrier islands. To build houses, hotels, and roads for them, developers flatten the dunes. As they fill in mud flats and marshes, they bury the plants growing there. As they change the islands, developers increase the erosion that occurs.

Some communities try to stop this erosion through "beach nourishment." This involves dumping many truckloads of sand on eroding beaches. However, without dunes to break the wind and plants to hold the sand in place, erosion continues. The new sand is soon washed away.

Erosion has caused many changes in the islands. For example, the Cape Hatteras Lighthouse had to be moved. The beach where it had stood since the 1800s had eroded. The lighthouse was in danger of falling into the ocean. In 1999, it was moved about one-half mile inland.

Erosion may eventually destroy the barrier islands. We need to learn better ways to deal with this relentless force so we can preserve these sandy national treasures.

Using a Rubric

A rubric is a tool for evaluating a piece of writing. To use a rubric, you assign 1, 2, 3, or 4 points to tell how well the author handled certain writing tasks. Remember the questions you read on page 182? Those questions were used to make this rubric.

"¡Buenos días! My name is Carlos. I just finished reading the report on page 183. Now I'm going to assess it using this rubric. First, I'll read the questions and the information for each question. Would you like to do it with me? After I assess that cause-and-effect report, I'm going to write my own report. You can, too."

Audience

Does the writer grab and hold the audience's attention?

Organization

Does the writer organize the report so it follows a cause-and-effect pattern?

Elaboration

Does the writer include supporting facts and reasons?

Clarification

Does the writer avoid using sentences that are too long and confusing?

Conventions & Skills

Does the writer use subject and object pronouns correctly, especially *who* and *whom*?

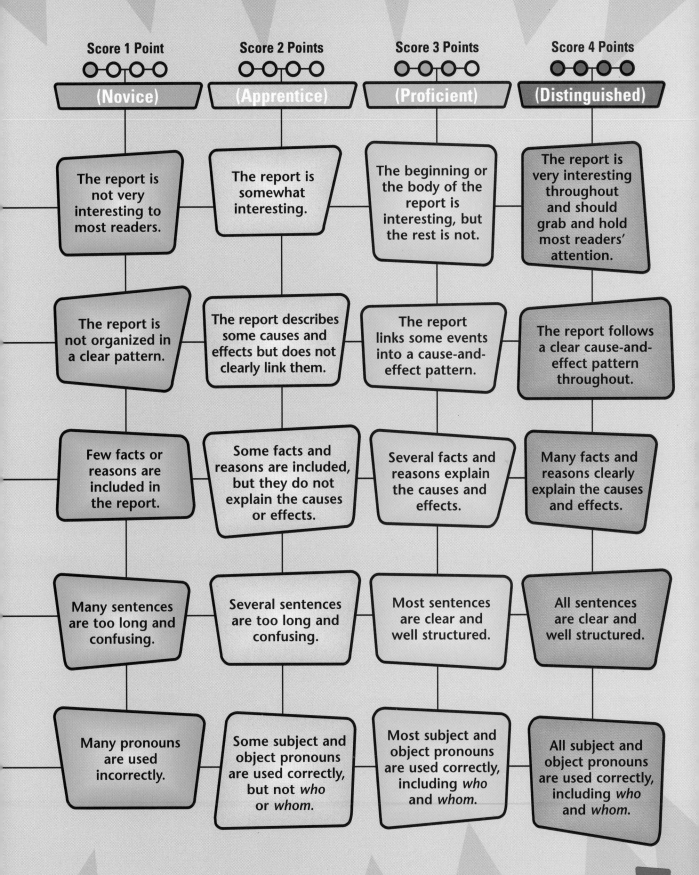

Score 1 Point (Novice)	Score 2 Points (Apprentice)	Score 3 Points (Proficient)	Score 4 Points (Distinguished)
The report is not very interesting to most readers.	The report is somewhat interesting.	The beginning or the body of the report is interesting, but the rest is not.	The report is very interesting throughout and should grab and hold most readers' attention.
The report is not organized in a clear pattern.	The report describes some causes and effects but does not clearly link them.	The report links some events into a cause-and-effect pattern.	The report follows a clear cause-and-effect pattern throughout.
Few facts or reasons are included in the report.	Some facts and reasons are included, but they do not explain the causes or effects.	Several facts and reasons explain the causes and effects.	Many facts and reasons clearly explain the causes and effects.
Many sentences are too long and confusing.	Several sentences are too long and confusing.	Most sentences are clear and well structured.	All sentences are clear and well structured.
Many pronouns are used incorrectly.	Some subject and object pronouns are used correctly, but not *who* or *whom*.	Most subject and object pronouns are used correctly, including *who* and *whom*.	All subject and object pronouns are used correctly, including *who* and *whom*.

Using a Rubric

to Study the Model

Use the rubric to evaluate Julia Tazzi's cause-and-effect report. Discuss each question on the rubric with your classmates. Find words and sentences in the report that help you answer each question.

Does the writer grab and hold the audience's attention?

> " The writer grabs my attention with her first sentence. I wondered why the islands are called 'children of the sea.' She also writes that the islands stretch for more than 100 miles and are centuries old, but they're in danger today. That's pretty wild. I wanted to keep reading. "

The barrier islands are called the "children of the sea." Born after the last ice age, they stretch along the Atlantic coast in long, narrow chains. Some of these chains extend for 100 miles or more. The islands have been around for nearly 18 centuries, but they may not exist forever.

Does the writer organize the report so it follows a cause-and-effect pattern?

" This report clearly explains the causes that created the barrier islands. The author also describes the effects of natural and people-caused erosion on the islands. For example, I could easily pick out the causes and effects in this paragraph. "

What caused the islands to form? At the end of the ice age, the air warmed and the glaciers melted. The melting ice caused rivers and streams to rise. As they flooded over the beaches, they carried sand and sediment to shallow areas just off the Atlantic coast. Ridges formed there. Then waves deposited more sand on the ridges. The ridges slowly became islands. Ocean currents pushed the sand up and down the islands. That caused them to lengthen into narrow strips.

Does the writer include supporting facts and reasons?

" The writer includes all sorts of facts and reasons to explain the causes and effects in her report. One fact that stood out for me was the need to move the Cape Hatteras Lighthouse. Erosion must have really washed away the beach around that lighthouse! I bet it was hard to move, too! "

Erosion has caused many changes in the islands. For example, the Cape Hatteras Lighthouse had to be moved. The beach where it had stood since the 1800s had eroded. The lighthouse was in danger of falling into the ocean. In 1999, it was moved about one-half mile inland.

Does the writer avoid using sentences that are too long and confusing?

" The author made her sentences easy to understand by not making them long and confusing. If she would have connected the sentences below with **ands,** I would have quit reading before I got to the end. The shorter, clearer sentences are much easier to read. "

The barrier islands have broad beaches and dunes on the ocean side. They have mud flats and salt marshes on the mainland side. This low, sandy structure is vulnerable to erosion.

Does the writer use subject and object pronouns correctly, especially *who* and *whom*?

" This author can handle pronouns! In this part, for example, she uses **who,** not **whom,** as the subject of the verb **enjoy.** Then she uses **them,** not **they,** as the object of the preposition **for.** That's tricky! "

Natural erosion isn't the only danger to these islands. People **who** enjoy the beach love to vacation on the barrier islands. To build houses, hotels, and roads for **them,** developers flatten the dunes.

" **Now it's my turn to write!**

I'm going to write a cause-and-effect report! I'm just learning how to do it, so I'll use the rubric and the model to help me. Follow along and learn with me. "

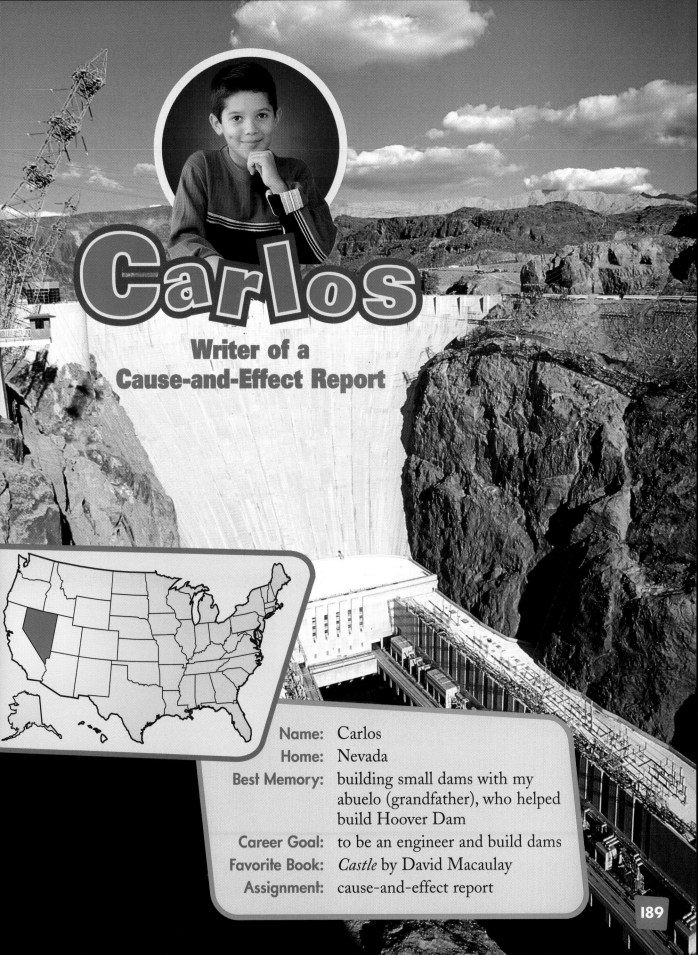

Carlos

**Writer of a
Cause-and-Effect Report**

Name: Carlos
Home: Nevada
Best Memory: building small dams with my abuelo (grandfather), who helped build Hoover Dam
Career Goal: to be an engineer and build dams
Favorite Book: *Castle* by David Macaulay
Assignment: cause-and-effect report

Prewriting

Gather

Choose my topic. Use the Internet to find two credible sources of information. Take notes.

" When our teacher asked us to write a cause-and-effect report, I thought for a while about my topic. Then I chose one that really interests me: dams and irrigation. I'd like to help build dams someday.

"I found two good sources for my topic on the Internet. My teacher says we can trust a Web site run by a government agency, most news organizations, an encyclopedia, or an educational organization (like a university or a museum).

"However, some sites might not be good. They might tell only one side of the story—part of the truth. Someone's personal Web site might not have the correct facts. Some sites are too complicated for me to understand. Other sites are out of date. I need up-to-date information! "

Credible Source

A **credible source** is a reliable place to obtain information. A credible source can be trusted to have accurate, unbiased, up-to-date information. School librarians can help you find credible sources if you need some guidance.

"Then I carefully took notes from my sources. I put the notes for each source on a separate sheet of paper. You can see some of my notes below. I found other sources, too, so I will have more pages of notes for my report.

"I might not use all the facts in these notes. I will choose the ones that best explain the causes and effects in my report."

Notes From the US Geological Service—Water Science for Schools: Irrigation Water Use

http://ga.water.usgs.gov/edu/wuir.html

1. About 60 percent of the world's fresh water is used for irrigation.

2. About 39 percent of the fresh water used in the United States is used to irrigate crops.

3. Farms could not feed the world without irrigation from rivers, lakes, reservoirs, and wells.

4. Of the water used for flood irrigation, one half is lost through evaporation or in transit (leaking pipes).

Notes From Colorado River Water Users Association: Nevada

http://crwua.mwd.dst.ca.us/nv/crwua_nv.htm

1. Nevada gets less rainfall than any other state, an average of 9 inches a year.

2. Building Hoover Dam on the Colorado River near the border of Nevada and Arizona increased the water supply for southern Nevada.

3. Hoover Dam created Lake Mead, one of the largest artificial lakes in the world.

4. Hoover Dam supplies electric power for Arizona, California, and Nevada.

Go to page 102 in the **Practice the Strategy Notebook!**

Prewriting

Organize

Make a cause-and-effect chain to organize my notes.

" As I looked over my notes, I noticed how some things cause other things. For example, Nevada gets little rain, so our farmers have to use irrigation.

"The **Rubric** reminds me to organize my report into a cause-and-effect pattern. This kind of pattern will help me show what causes what. I know that sometimes one cause has several effects, like when a storm blows down trees, causes rivers to overflow, and brings lightning.

"Other times, several causes lead to the same effect. One example I can think of is when you pay attention in class, read the assigned chapters, and do your other homework. What's the effect? You get good grades! (You also learn more, of course!)

"Anyway, a cause-and-effect chain shows how events connect. The effect of one event can become the cause of the next event. The events link together in a chain.

"Organizing my notes into a cause-and-effect chain will help me explain how one action or event leads to the next one. You can see part of my chain on the next page. Some of my classmates made two or three chains for their reports. Each chain was for a different main idea. "

Cause-and-Effect Chain

A **cause-and-effect chain** shows actions and their results. One effect can have several causes, and one cause can have several effects.

Cause

Not enough rain falls in the U.S. where many crops are grown.

Effect/Cause

About 39% of fresh water in U.S. is used for irrigation.

Effect/Cause

About half of the water used in flood irrigation is lost.

Effect/Cause

Farmers are turning to more efficient irrigation methods.

Effect

Drip irrigation is being used for fruits and vegetables.

Effect

Spray irrigation is being used on large farms.

Go to page 104 in the **Practice** the Strategy **Notebook!**

Drafting

Write
Draft my report. Show how each cause leads to an effect.

      Now it's time to start writing. I'll use my cause-and-effect chain to show how each cause leads to an effect. I'll add facts and details along the way.

    "I'll also think of a way to begin that grabs the attention of my audience—my classmates, in this case. They may not have to irrigate crops, but they do live in Nevada, where water is scarce. I'll start with a question that gets them thinking about how we use our water. Then I'll include interesting facts that will keep them reading.

    "I'll do my best with spelling and grammar now and check for mistakes later. Looking up hard-to-spell words in a dictionary would interrupt my concentration. I'll do that when I edit my final draft.

    "You can read the beginning of my draft on the next page. What do you think so far?

interesting introduction
↓

Do you know how nearly 40 percent of the fresh water in the United States is used? It's not used for drinking or baths or swimming pools. It's used for irrigation! Many areas in the United States don't get enough rainfall to grow crops, so the land must be irrigated.

Most irrigation is in the Western states, where it's bone dry water is scarce. Believe it or not You probably already know that Nevada **cause** gets less rainfall than any other state, so farmers here depend on irrigation to grow their crops. ← **effect**

The oldest and cheapest type of irrigation is flood irrigation. In this method, water is allowed to flow along rows of plants. However, about half of the water used in this type of irrigation evaporates or runs off the fields. To keep water from running off their fields, farmers whom live in hilly areas make there fields as level as possible. They also release water at intervals. This reduces runoff, too. In addition, some farmers capture the runoff in ponds. There it is stored for they to use again.

cause →
To conserve water, people farmers across the West have experimented with other methods of irrigation. Many of they now use more **effect** → efficient methods. Farmers whom are challenged by the Nevada desert must be especially careful. Nevada potato farmers, in particular, need to irrigate their fields. Potatoes need seven times more water than crops like wheat!

Go to page 108 in the **Practice the Strategy Notebook!**

Revising

Elaborate — Add supporting facts and reasons.

" When you write a report, you can't expect readers to believe that something is true just because you say it is. You have to support what you say with facts that can be proven and reasons why something happens. The **Rubric** reminds me that I need plenty of those, so I added some to this paragraph—and in other places in my report, too. I think they made my report much more convincing. "

Reason

A **reason** is the explanation behind an act, idea, or opinion. For example, one reason to wear a coat outdoors is that the temperature is only 40 degrees.

[2nd DRAFT]

— added reason why water evaporates

   Spray irrigation is used on many large farms. When older machinery is used, most of the water evaporates into the air because water shoots through the air onto the ground. Newer machinery gently sprays water from a hanging pipe onto the ground. Little of it evaporates.

added fact → Farmers who use the newer machinery conserve water. They can increase their irrigation efficiency from 60 percent to 90 percent.

Go to page 111 in the **Practice** the Strategy **Notebook!**

Revising

Clarify
Rewrite sentences that are too long and confusing.

" I read the second draft of my report to my friend, Eric. He can tell when something isn't quite clear. He pointed out the long, confusing sentence in this paragraph. I divided it into three sentences! Now it's easier to read and understand, don't you think? I bet I can find more long sentences in my report and divide them, too. "

[3rd DRAFT]

Many farmers, including those in Nevada, now use drip irrigation for fruits and vegetables. The water runs through plastic pipes laid along crop rows or buried in the soil. and holes in the pipes allow the water to drip directly into the soil. and the water soaks into the ground instead of running off or evaporating.

revised long sentence

Go to page 112 in the **Practice** the Strategy **Notebook!**

Expository Writing • Cause-and-Effect Report

Editing

Proofread

Check to see that subject and object pronouns have been used correctly, especially *who* and *whom*.

> Okay, it's time to do the nitty-gritty stuff—spelling, grammar, and punctuation. I have to double-check that I used subject and object pronouns correctly. I have problems with **who** and **whom,** especially.

Conventions & SKILLS

Subject and Object Pronouns

- A **subject pronoun** takes the place of the subject in a sentence.

  Example: We have been irrigating crops for thousands of years.

- An **object pronoun** replaces the object of a verb or a preposition.

  Example: Irrigation helps **us** feed Earth's people.

- Use *who* as a subject pronoun. Use *whom* as an object pronoun.

  Example: People **who** build dams are skilled workers **whom** we respect. (*Who* is the subject of the verb *build*. *Whom* is the object of the verb *respect*.)

Extra Practice

See **Subject and Object Pronouns** (pages CS 18–CS 19) in the back of this book.

" Here's part of my fourth draft, so you can see the kinds of errors
I corrected. "

[4th DRAFT]

changed to a subject pronoun

The oldest and cheapest type of irrigation is flood irrigation. In this method, water is allowed to flow along rows of plants. However, about half of the water used in this type of irrigation evaporates or runs off the fields. To keep water from running off their fields, farmers ~~whom~~ who live in hilly areas make their fields as level as possible.

They also release water at intervals. This reduces runoff, too. In addition, some farmers capture the runoff in ponds. There it is stored for ~~they~~ them to use again. **changed to an object pronoun**

To conserve water, farmers across the West have experimented with other methods of irrigation. Many of ~~they~~ them now use more efficient methods. Farmers ~~whom~~ who are challenged by the Nevada desert must be especially careful. Nevada potato farmers, in particular, need to irrigate their fields. Potatoes need seven times more water than crops like wheat!

Go to page 113 in the **Practice** the Strategy **Notebook!**

Publishing

Share   Add my cause-and-effect report to a class binder.

Writer:	Carlos
Assignment:	cause-and-effect report
Topic:	irrigation in Nevada
Audience:	classmates
Method of Publication:	binder of class reports titled "Why Does That Happen?"
Reason for Choice:	We're learning more about writing cause-and-effect reports by reading each other's reports.

"Our class wants to get better at writing cause-and-effect reports because we write them in many classes. We decided to put all our reports in one binder. That way, we can read each other's reports and learn from them. Here's how I got my report ready to put in the binder."

1. First, I checked my report one more time for mistakes.

2. I thought of a title that fits our class binder title and added my name as author.

3. Then I made a clean copy of my report.

4. I punched holes in the report and added it to the class binder.

Why Are Nevada's Crops Irrigated?

by Carlos

Do you know how almost 40 percent of the fresh water in the United States is used? It's not used for drinking or baths or swimming pools. It's used for irrigation! Many areas in the United States don't get enough rainfall to grow crops. That land must be irrigated.

Most irrigation is in the Western states, where water is scarce. You probably already know that Nevada gets less rainfall than any other state, so farmers here depend on irrigation to grow their crops. In our state, 67 percent of all cropland requires irrigation. In fact, the U.S. government's first irrigation project was in Nevada.

The oldest and cheapest type of irrigation is flood irrigation. In this method, water is allowed to flow along rows of plants. However, about half of the water used in this type of irrigation evaporates or runs off the fields. To keep water from running off their fields, farmers who live in hilly areas make their fields as level as possible. They also release water at intervals. This reduces runoff, too. In addition, some farmers capture the runoff in ponds. There it is stored for them to use again.

To conserve water, farmers across the West have experimented with other methods of irrigation. Many of them now use more efficient methods. Farmers who are challenged by the Nevada desert must be especially careful. Nevada potato farmers, in particular, need to irrigate their fields. Potatoes need seven times more water than crops like wheat!

Many farmers, including those in Nevada, now use drip irrigation for fruits and vegetables. The water runs through plastic pipes laid along crop rows or buried in the soil. Holes in the pipes allow the water to drip directly into the soil. The water soaks into the ground instead of running off or evaporating.

Spray irrigation is used on many large farms. When older machinery is used, most of the water evaporates into the air because water shoots through the air onto the ground. Newer machinery gently sprays water from a hanging pipe onto the ground. Little of it evaporates. Farmers who use the newer machinery conserve water. They can increase their irrigation efficiency from 60 percent to 90 percent.

In Nevada, if you want to grow crops, you must irrigate!

USING the Rubric for Assessment

Go to page 114 in the **Practice** the Strategy **Notebook!** Use that rubric to assess Carlos's report. Try using the rubric to assess your own writing.

EXPOSITORY writing

Research Report

In this chapter, you will work with one kind of expository writing: a **research report**.

In writing a **research report,** the writer gathers information, organizes it, and explains the main points to readers. The writer should use multiple sources to gather facts about the topic and then cite (or identify) those sources in the report.

Beginning on the next page is a research report. Read the questions below. Then read the report, keeping the questions in mind.

Does the writer present the audience with interesting information about a specific topic?

Does the writer organize the body of the report by writing one or more paragraphs about each main point?

Does the writer add to the report by including an introduction that states the topic in an interesting way and a conclusion that summarizes the main points?

Does the writer use the active voice whenever possible?

Does the writer correctly capitalize and punctuate proper nouns and proper adjectives?

Digging Into Backyard Archaeology

by Peter Nuan

With a toothbrush, Jan Haas carefully removed dirt from a little lump in her hand. The object under the dirt glinted in the sunlight. Was it a piece of gold jewelry? She continued to brush off the soil hiding the object. The shape became clear. It was round and fairly flat. Then she saw a design. Soon it was clear that the object was a tarnished brass button.

It had been buried six inches deep in Jan's backyard in Baltimore, Maryland. She dug it up near an old wash house. The wash house had been built in the mid-1700s. Later, Jan learned the button was from the Colonial period.

As a backyard archaeologist, Jan was pleased with her find. Backyard archaeologists are amateurs. Like the professionals, they search for and study objects made by people long ago.

Across America, people like Jan Haas are digging up their backyards. They hope to find treasures. These treasures will probably not be gold or diamonds. More likely, they will be old buttons or chipped glass. They still are valuable, though. They tell about an area's history and culture. A dig in the backyards of Alexandria, Virginia, uncovered items from more than a century ago. They included marbles, medicine bottles, and pottery shards. Before the Civil War, free African Americans lived in the area. "By studying these artifacts, we were able to trace the development of this neighborhood and the lifestyles of its inhabitants," said the city's archaeologist, Pamela J. Cressey, Ph.D.

Archaeologists urge people who dig as a hobby to follow a few guidelines. If amateurs just start digging, they may destroy valuable old objects.

First, property owners should research their site. Town records may provide useful facts about former owners. News clippings and photos may also be helpful. Many libraries and museums may have collections of these clippings. Information about early Native American groups living in the region is usually available at history museums.

Backyard archaeologists should then contact authorities and explain what they have learned about the site. The state archaeologist is a good person to contact. Other possible contacts are historical societies and college archaeology departments. An expert will often arrange a survey of the site.

Some backyard sites contain valuable objects. Unless such a site is in danger of being destroyed, archaeologists usually ask property owners not to dig there. They believe the past should be left untouched so it will be preserved for the future. If the site is in danger, the archaeologists may conduct a dig. They often ask the property owner to help.

Whatever diggers find at the site belongs to the property owners. Some backyard archaeologists donate the items to a historical society or museum. There, trained professionals can catalog and care for the items. Objects removed from the ground may dry out, rot, or get moldy. Professionals know how to preserve these objects. They can keep them safe for study and display.

Some backyard archaeologists get started by volunteering at a dig site. Several government agencies offer a chance to work in the field. For example, Passport in Time (PIT) is a volunteer program of the U.S. Forest Service. Its aim is to preserve landmarks in national forests. PIT volunteers work with archaeologists on sites around the country. Linda Ruys is a teacher who volunteered at a PIT site in the Allegheny National Forest in Pennsylvania. She said, "The work is long, over 40 hours per week in a hot, bug-infested atmosphere. The buckets are heavy, the shovel too, but the rewards are great and the friendships lasting."

School programs are another place to learn the basics of archaeology. Sixth-grade students at Blake Middle School in Medfield, Massachusetts, learn through a hands-on experience. Each fall they work in teams on an old trash heap owned by a local family. They have found old nails, jars, and pieces of an old toy bank.

The students learn to use the correct tools and methods. They are shown how to mark the site into square plots. They learn how to properly dig with a trowel. They also practice sifting buckets of soil through screens. Any objects in the soil remain on the screen while the dirt falls through. Finally, they learn to record what they find and where they find it.

Another place to learn about archaeology is a Web site called "Dr. Dig." This Web site gives advice about backyard archaeology. For example, Dr. Dig stresses that diggers should consider every item to be important. "...the crummy fragment of bone is just the bit of evidence that proves the date of the monument or some other piece of valuable information about the site," says Dr. Dig.

Archaeology requires patience and attention to detail. It requires caring about the past and the future. Many backyard archaeologists love their hobby for these reasons. Some professional archaeologists worry about what might be lost if the amateurs are not careful. However, amateurs can learn how to dig the right way by consulting experts and working as volunteers in the field. As Dr. Dig might say, every tarnished button counts.

Sources

"Archaeology." *Encyclopedia Britannica*. 2001 ed.

"Ask Dr. Dig." Dr. Dig, 2000.
  http://dig.archaeology.org/drdig/digging/

Atkin, Ross. "Kids dig history." *Christian Science Monitor*. 23 Nov. 1999; 22.

Haas, Jan. Personal interview. 12 Sept. 2001.

Proeller, Marie. "Backyard Archaeology." *Country Living*. Aug. 1998; 40.

Ruys, Linda. "Dig This Experience." Passport in Time: A Volunteer Program of the USDA Forest Service. PIT Projects from Previous Seasons, Pennsylvania, 1997.
  www.passportintime.com/summaries/pa97a_buckaloons.html

"Welcome to Passport in Time!" Passport in Time: A Volunteer Program of the USDA Forest Service.
  www.passportintime.com/

Using a Rubric

You know that a rubric is a tool that lists "what counts" for a piece of writing. You assign 1, 2, 3, or 4 points to tell how well the author handled certain writing tasks.

Remember the questions you read on page 202? Those questions were used to make this rubric.

"Hey there, I'm Maya. What did you think of the research report on the last few pages? Do you want to see how I assess it? I'm going to use this rubric. First, I'll read the questions and the information for each question. Then I'll assess the report. Afterward, I'll write a research report of my own. I'll bet you'll be writing one soon, too."

Audience

Does the writer present the audience with interesting information about a specific topic?

Organization

Does the writer organize the body of the report by writing one or more paragraphs about each main point?

Elaboration

Does the writer add to the report by including an introduction that states the topic in an interesting way and a conclusion that summarizes the main points?

Clarification

Does the writer use the active voice whenever possible?

Conventions & Skills

Does the writer correctly capitalize and punctuate proper nouns and proper adjectives?

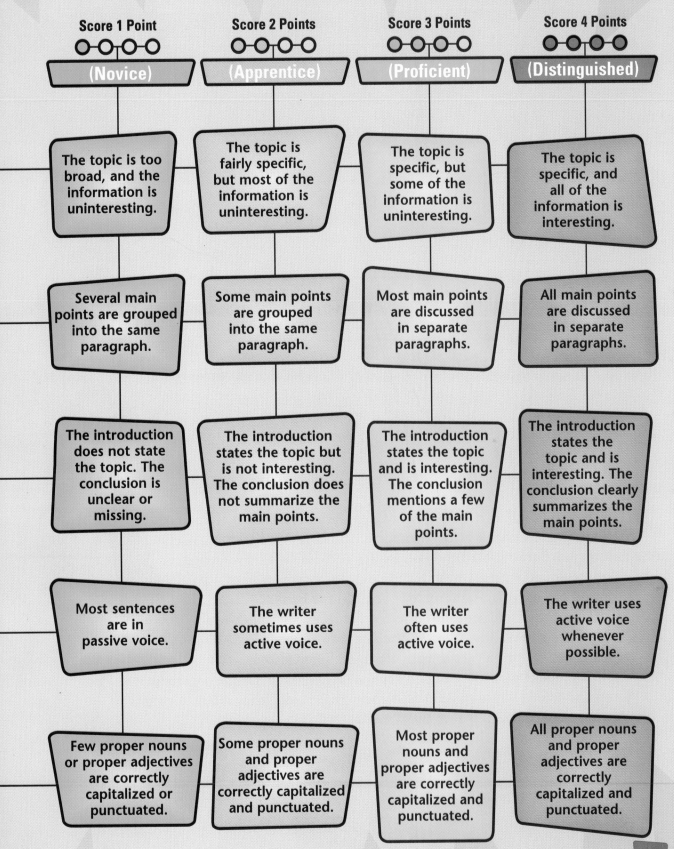

Score 1 Point (Novice)	Score 2 Points (Apprentice)	Score 3 Points (Proficient)	Score 4 Points (Distinguished)
The topic is too broad, and the information is uninteresting.	The topic is fairly specific, but most of the information is uninteresting.	The topic is specific, but some of the information is uninteresting.	The topic is specific, and all of the information is interesting.
Several main points are grouped into the same paragraph.	Some main points are grouped into the same paragraph.	Most main points are discussed in separate paragraphs.	All main points are discussed in separate paragraphs.
The introduction does not state the topic. The conclusion is unclear or missing.	The introduction states the topic but is not interesting. The conclusion does not summarize the main points.	The introduction states the topic and is interesting. The conclusion mentions a few of the main points.	The introduction states the topic and is interesting. The conclusion clearly summarizes the main points.
Most sentences are in passive voice.	The writer sometimes uses active voice.	The writer often uses active voice.	The writer uses active voice whenever possible.
Few proper nouns or proper adjectives are correctly capitalized or punctuated.	Some proper nouns and proper adjectives are correctly capitalized and punctuated.	Most proper nouns and proper adjectives are correctly capitalized and punctuated.	All proper nouns and proper adjectives are correctly capitalized and punctuated.

Using a Rubric to Study the Model

Use the rubric to evaluate Peter Nuan's research report. Discuss each question with your classmates. Find words and sentences in the report that help you answer each question.

Audience

Does the writer present the audience with interesting information about a specific topic?

" I didn't know anything about backyard archaeology, but the writer told me all about it and explained how I could learn more, too. All the information was interesting, but I especially liked the paragraphs below. They made me realize that kids can do backyard archaeology, too. "

School programs are another place to learn the basics of archaeology. Sixth-grade students at Blake Middle School in Medfield, Massachusetts, learn through a hands-on experience. Each fall they work in teams on an old trash heap owned by a local family. They have found old nails, jars, and pieces of an old toy bank.

The students learn to use the correct tools and methods. They are shown how to mark the site into square plots. They learn how to properly dig with a trowel. They also practice sifting buckets of soil through screens. Any objects in the soil remain on the screen while the dirt falls through. Finally, they learn to record what they find and where they find it.

Organization

Does the writer organize the body of the report by writing one or more paragraphs about each main point?

> The writer explains each main point in its own paragraph. That makes his report easy to understand. Here he tells how people can find out more about a backyard site.

First, property owners should research their site. Town records may provide useful facts about former owners. News clippings and photos may also be helpful. Many libraries and museums may have collections of these clippings. Information about early Native American groups living in the region is usually available at history museums.

Elaboration

Does the writer add to the report by including an introduction that states the topic in an interesting way and a conclusion that summarizes the main points?

> The introduction interested me right away. I wanted to know what Jan found. Then the conclusion sums everything up.

With a toothbrush, Jan Haas carefully removed dirt from a little lump in her hand. The object under the dirt glinted in the sunlight. Was it a piece of gold jewelry? She continued to brush off the soil hiding the object. The shape became clear. It was round and fairly flat. Then she saw a design. Soon it was clear that the object was a tarnished brass button.

Archaeology requires patience and attention to detail. It requires caring about the past and the future. Many backyard archaeologists love their hobby for these reasons. Some professional archaeologists worry about what might be lost if the amateurs are not careful. However, amateurs can learn how to dig the right way by consulting experts and working as volunteers in the field. As Dr. Dig might say, every tarnished button counts.

Does the writer use the active voice whenever possible?

❝This writer could have used mostly passive voice, like this: 'The items are donated by some backyard archaeologists to a historical society or museum. There, the items can be cataloged and cared for by trained professionals.'

"Instead, he uses active voice. See how he does it? The sentences are much clearer in active voice.❞

Some backyard archaeologists donate the items to a historical society or museum. There, trained professionals can catalog and care for the items.

Does the writer correctly capitalize and punctuate proper nouns and proper adjectives?

Yes! Look how many different proper nouns and proper adjectives he had to deal with in this paragraph.

A dig in the backyards of Alexandria, Virginia, uncovered items from more than a century ago. They included marbles, medicine bottles, and pottery shards. Before the Civil War, free African Americans lived in the area. "By studying these artifacts, we were able to trace the development of this neighborhood and the lifestyles of its inhabitants," said the city's archaeologist, Pamela J. Cressey, Ph.D.

❝**Now it's my turn to write!**

I'm going to write a research report on my own topic. With the help of the rubric and the model, I think I'll write a pretty good one. You can follow along and see how I do.❞

MaYA

Writer of a Research Report

Name: Maya

Home: Washington, D.C.

Hobbies: cooking and acting

Career Goal: to have my own TV cooking show or be an actress

Favorite Book: *Out of the Dust* by Karen Hesse

Assignment: research report

Prewriting

Gather

Choose my topic. Look it up in an encyclopedia to narrow the topic. Check two other sources and make note cards.

" As soon as I heard we were going to write research reports, I thought of India, where my family used to live. I figured there was a lot about India that would be interesting to my classmates. They will be my audience.

"However, when I looked up the word **India** in an encyclopedia, I found a LONG list of topics. They included India's people, geography, climate, natural resources, religions, history, government—the list went on and on. I needed to narrow my topic!

"I skimmed the section about the people of India. One item caught my eye: the food they eat. I'm learning to cook Indian food, so I wanted to know more about it. Still, even Indian food turned out to be too broad a topic. There are so many kinds!

"I learned from the encyclopedia that people in different parts of India eat different dishes. I decided to narrow down my topic to regional foods of India. I think my classmates will find that interesting. They love anything to do with food! "

❝ In addition to the encyclopedia, I checked two other sources. As I read, I took notes on note cards. Each card had one piece of information and its source. Here are two of my note cards. **❞**

Note Card

A **note card,** usually an index card, should include the topic, information about the topic (either summarized or directly quoted), and the source of the information. Use one note card for each piece of information.

Regional Food in India—South India

source: "Regional Food." Indian Food Reference Guide. www.sanjeevkapoor.com/reference/regional/regionalfood.html

"Rice is the staple food and is cooked in a variety of ways. Dosas (shallow fried paper-thin pancakes) and idlis (steamed dumplings) are the most famous South Indian dishes."

Regional Food in India—Introduction

source: Kanitkar, V.P. Indian Food and Drink. New York: Bookwright Press, 1987.

Religion and climate are two things that determine food habits in each region.

Go to page 116 in the **Practice** the Strategy **Notebook!**

Prewriting

Organize

Make an outline to organize my notes.

"The best way to organize my report is to organize my notes, right? I considered several different graphic organizers and decided to use an outline to organize the body of my report. That way, I can put details under the main points. Then I'll write one or two paragraphs about each main point and its details. I'll write the introduction and conclusion of my report later.

"To get started, I made a separate pile of note cards for each main point. Then I wrote the outline you see below and on the next page. I decided to use a sentence outline instead of a topic outline."

Outline

An **outline** organizes notes by main points and supporting details. Each main point has a Roman numeral. The supporting details under each main point have capital letters. Any information listed under a supporting detail gets a number. In a sentence outline, all the information is in complete sentences. In a topic outline, words and phrases are used.

I. Regional foods are determined by many things.

    A. One main influence is religion.

        1. Most people are vegetarian hindus.

        2. Immigrants from other religions who eat meat influence the hindu diet.

    B. India's many different climates also affect food production.

II. The North has a strong muslim influence.

    A. Muslims live in the North.

        1. They eat lamb, chicken, beef and fish.

        2. Many do not eat pork.

    B. Dates, nuts, and milk are used in sweets.

    C. Hindu bread and vegetarian dishes are also common.

III. Food in the South has a more traditional hindu style.

    A. Rice is cooked in many ways.

    B. The two most famous dishes are dosas and idlis.

    C. Vegetables served with rice include soupy dishes made from peas or beans.

IV. Coastal Indian food has many influences.

    A. Fish dishes are common and varied.

    B. They include carp with chilies, prawns with mustard seed, and fish curry.

    C. Some foods are made with coconut.

Go to page 119 in the **Practice** the Strategy **Notebook!**

Drafting

Write

Draft the body of my report. Write at least one paragraph for every main point on my outline.

"I'm ready to roll! I've got a good outline that organizes my notes. Now I will write one or two paragraphs for each point in my outline—just like it says in the **Rubric**. That will be the body of my report. Later, I'll add an introduction and a conclusion.

"I'm going to concentrate on getting all this information down on paper now. I'll do my best with spelling and grammar and check for mistakes later. You can read part of my report on these two pages. Can you see how my outline helped me organize my information?"

Body

The **body** is the main part of your report. The body comes between the introduction and conclusion and develops your main points.

[ist DRAFT]

main point (I.)

first supporting detail (A.)

~~What people~~ The foods people eat in each region of India are determined by many things. Religion is a big thing. In India, ~~there are~~ 80 percent of the population is hindu and strict hindus are vegetarians and do not eat meat. Immigrants who practice other religions have come to India. Many of these people do eat meat. They have influenced the traditional hindu diet in some places.

I.

Another big thing is climate. The ~~type of~~ food production of a region is affected by the climate there. For example, rice is grown

second paragraph on the same main point; second supporting detail (B.)

mostly in the tropical south and the rainy northeast and wheat is an important crop in the dry northern plains.

main point (II.) →

~~In the north~~ The North has a strong muslim influence. Muslims eat lamb, chicken, beef, and fish but not pork. One favorite dish is lamb kebab. Lamb kebab is pieces of mildly spiced meat roasted on skewers. Another favorite is tandoori chicken, spiced chicken cooked in a clay oven. Dates, nuts, and milk are in many deserts called milk sweets. The milk comes from water buffalos. They are the main source of milk in India. Kheer is a milk sweet similar to rice pudding.

second paragraph about the same main point; supporting detail (C.)

II.-

Bread and vegetarian dishes from the hindu tradition are also common in the North. ~~The~~ Most breads don't have any yeast, so they don't rise. Parathas are flat ~~kind of~~ cakes of wheat dough baked on a hot stone and then pan-fried. Purees are flat circles of wheat dough deep-fried in oil until they puff up like balloons. A ~~really good~~ dish of spiced rice and vegetables called pullao is also popular. In the North, the pullao vegetables are usually cauliflower and peas.

Food ~~from the~~ in the South has a more traditional hindu style. Rice is used all the time and it's cooked in lots of different ways. ~~The author who wrote~~ V P (Hemant) Kanitkar, author of <u>Indian Food and Drink</u>, says "Rice grains, simply boiled may appear to us to be a poor meal, but different processes like grinding, pounding, steaming, and frying transform rice and other cereals into tasty dishes."

main point (III.)

III.-

second paragraph about the same main point; supporting detail (B.)

The two most famous South indian foods are made from rice. Dosas are thin rice-flour pancakes. Idlis are steamed rice dumplings. Vegetables served with rice include dal, soupy dishes made from split peas or beans.

Go to page 121 in the **Practice** the Strategy **Notebook!**

Revising

Elaborate

Add an introduction that states the topic and interests the reader. Add a conclusion that summarizes the main points.

❝I used my outline to write the body of my report. Then I added an introduction to grab my reader's attention. You can read it below.

"Then, because a research report is usually kind of long, I made sure my conclusion wrapped everything up. What do you think?❞

Introduction, Conclusion

A good **introduction** grabs the audience's attention and introduces the topic of the report. A **conclusion** ties up loose ends and summarizes the main points.

[2nd DRAFT]

introduction

Variety Is the Spice of Indian Food

WARNING: This report may cause an uncontrollable craving for indian food, such as samosas. A samosa is a deep-fried, triangular pastry stuffed with potatoes and other vegetables. Spices like chili powder and garlic give it zing. Samosas are a common dish in gujarat, one of India's many regions. People eat different types of foods in different regions of India.

The many regions of India offer a huge range of foods to try. Mostly that's because of religion and climate. Variety is the spice of indian food. Anyone who ignored the warning at the beginning of this report probably is ready to sample the many types of indian food now.

conclusion

Go to page 124 in the Practice the Strategy Notebook!

Revising

Clarify — Use active voice as much as possible.

66 The **Rubric** reminds me to use active voice as much as possible. As I read my report to myself, I realized I'm not using active voice as much as I could. In this paragraph, I changed passive voice to active voice in three sentences. It makes a difference, doesn't it? 99

READ TO MYSELF

Active Voice

A verb is in **active voice** if the subject of the sentence is doing the action. Using active voice makes your writing stronger and clearer. A verb is in passive voice if the subject is being acted upon.

Active Voice: George ate his lunch.

Passive Voice: The lunch was eaten by George.

[3rd DRAFT]

~~The foods people eat in each region of India are determined by~~
Many factors determine the foods people eat in each region of India.
~~many factors.~~ Religion is a major factor. In India, 80 percent of the population is hindu. Strict hindus are vegetarians and do not eat meat. Over the centuries, immigrants who practice other religions have come to India. Many of these people do eat meat. They have influenced the traditional hindu diet in some places.

changed passive voice to active voice

The climate of a region affects food production there.
Another major factor is climate. ~~Food production is affected by~~
people grow
~~the climate of a region.~~ For example, rice ~~is grown~~ mostly in the tropical south and the rainy northeast. Wheat is an important crop in the dry northern plains.

Go to page 126 in the **Practice** the Strategy **Notebook!**

Editing

Proofread

Check to see that I have correctly capitalized and punctuated proper nouns and proper adjectives.

"Now I will check my spelling, grammar, and punctuation. I used a lot of proper nouns and proper adjectives, so I'll make sure I capitalized and punctuated them right."

Conventions & Skills

Proper Nouns and Proper Adjectives

- Capitalize **proper nouns** (a specific person, place, thing, or idea).
  Example: India is as large as **Western Europe**.

- Capitalize **proper adjectives** (descriptive words formed from proper nouns).
  Example: I took an **Indian** cooking class.

- Capitalize **titles of respect** when they are used before a person's name.
  Example: Mr. Veenu Mukharji taught my cooking class.

- Capitalize **proper abbreviations** (words in addresses such as *street* and *avenue*, days, months, and parts of business names in informal notes). End the abbreviations with a period.
  Example: Indian Movie Production **Co.**, 414 Raj **St.**, Bhopal, India

- Capitalize an **initial** when it replaces the name of a person or place. Follow the initial with a period.
  Example: The movie *Swami and Friends* was based on **R. K.** Narayan's novel.

Extra Practice

See **Proper Nouns and Proper Adjectives** (pages CS 20–CS 21) in the back of this book.

Proofreading Marks

⊐ Indent.

≡ Make a capital.

/ Make a small letter.

⋀ Add something.

ℓ Take out something.

⊙ Add a period.

⌗ New paragraph

SP Spelling error

" Here's part of my fourth draft, so you can see the kinds of errors I corrected. "

[4th DRAFT]

Food in the southern part of India has a more traditional hindu **capitalized proper adjective**

style. Rice is prepared in many ways. V. P. (Hemant) Kanitkar, author **capitalized proper initials**

of Indian Food and Drink, says "Rice grains, simply boiled may

appear to us to be a poor meal, but different processes like grind-

ing, pounding, steaming, and frying transform rice and other cereals

into tasty dishes."

The two most famous South indian foods are made from rice. **capitalized proper adjective**

Dosas are thin rice-flour pancakes. Idlis are steamed rice

dumplings. Vegetables served with rice include dal, soupy dishes

made from split peas or beans.

Coastal Indian food has many influences. Naturally, people there

eat a lot of fish. The people of west Bengal live near rivers as well **capitalized proper nouns**

as the bay of Bengal. They enjoy carp cooked with chilies. Another

favorite bengali recipe is prawns. These large shrimp are spiced **capitalized proper adjectives**

with mustard seeds.

Goa has a strong portuguese influence. Its fish curries are well

known. A curry is a general term for a dish cooked with crushed

spices and turmeric. Turmeric is an herb that adds a yellow color.

Coconuts are plentyful in Kerala. Coconut milk is used in fish, rice,

and vegetable coconut curries.

Go to page 127 in the **Practice** the Strategy **Notebook!**

Publishing

Share

Include my written report as part of a multimedia presentation to the class.

Writer: Maya
Assignment: research report
Topic: food in India
Audience: classmates
Method of Publication: multimedia presentation
Reason for Choice: Using different media helps make our reports more interesting.

"Multimedia doesn't mean you have to use a computer, although I will. It just means that you present information in more than one way, like with pictures and sound.

"When I give my presentation, I'm going to offer samples of Indian food and play some Indian music low in the background. I'm also going to hand out maps showing the regions of India. Here's how I got ready to make my presentation."

1. First, I checked my research report one more time for mistakes.

2. Then I added my name as the author and made a clean copy.

3. I got my teacher's approval for each part of my presentation.

4. I found a computer picture to go with my report and helped my grandmother make Indian food for us.

5. Next, I practiced making my multimedia presentation, especially using the computer.

6. I made my presentation to the class. They loved it! (And the food, too!)

Variety Is the Spice of Indian Food

by Maya

WARNING: This report may cause an uncontrollable craving for Indian food, such as samosas. A samosa is a deep-fried, triangular pastry stuffed with potatoes and other vegetables. Spices like chili powder and garlic give it zing. Samosas are a common dish in Gujarat, one of India's many regions. People eat different types of foods in different regions of India.

Many factors determine the foods people eat in each region of India. Religion is a major factor. In India, 80 percent of the population is Hindu. Strict Hindus are vegetarians and do not eat meat. Over the centuries, immigrants who practice other religions have come to India. Many of these people do eat meat. They have influenced the traditional Hindu diet in some places.

Another major factor is climate. The climate of a region affects the food production there. For example, people grow rice mostly in the tropical South and the rainy Northeast. Wheat is an important crop in the dry northern plains.

The North has a strong Muslim influence. Muslims eat lamb, chicken, beef, and fish but not pork. One favorite dish is lamb kebab. Lamb kebab is pieces of mildly spiced meat roasted on skewers. Another favorite is tandoori chicken, spiced chicken cooked in a clay oven. Dates, nuts, and milk are in many desserts called milk sweets. The milk comes from water buffaloes. They are the main source of milk in India. Kheer is a milk sweet similar to rice pudding.

Bread and vegetarian dishes from the Hindu tradition are also common in the North. Most breads don't have any yeast, so they don't rise. Parathas are flat cakes of wheat dough baked on a hot stone and then pan-fried. Purees are flat circles of wheat dough deep-fried in oil until they puff up like balloons. A dish of spiced rice and vegetables called pullao is also popular. In the North, the pullao vegetables are usually cauliflower and peas.

Food in the South has a more traditional Hindu style.

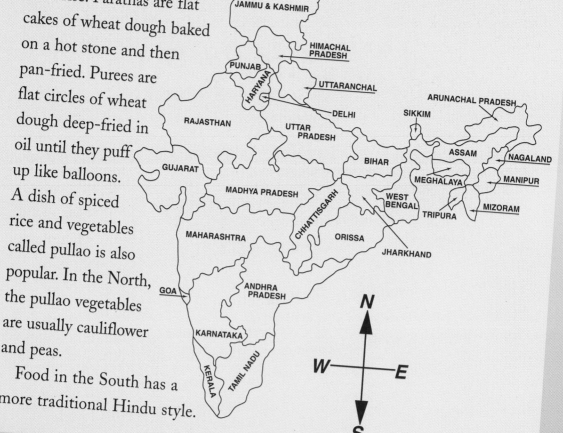

Expository Writing • Research Report

Rice is prepared in many ways. V. P. (Hemant) Kanitkar, author of *Indian Food and Drink,* says, "Rice grains, simply boiled may appear to us to be a poor meal, but different processes like grinding, pounding, steaming, and frying transform rice and other cereals into tasty dishes."

The two most famous South Indian foods are made from rice. Dosas are thin rice-flour pancakes. Idlis are steamed rice dumplings. Vegetables served with rice include dal, soupy dishes made from split peas or beans.

Coastal Indian food has many influences. Naturally, people there eat a lot of fish. The people of West Bengal live near rivers as well as the Bay of Bengal. They enjoy carp cooked with chilies. Another favorite Bengali recipe is prawns. These large shrimp are spiced with mustard seeds.

Goa has a strong Portuguese influence. Its fish curries are well known. A curry is a general term for a dish cooked with crushed spices and turmeric. Turmeric is an herb that adds a yellow color. Coconuts are plentiful in Kerala. Coconut milk is used in fish, rice, and vegetable coconut curries.

Because of the influence of religion and climate, the many regions of India offer a huge range of foods. Variety is the spice of Indian food. Those who ignored the warning at the beginning of this report will now probably be eager to sample the many types of Indian food.

Sources

"India." *The World Book Encyclopedia.* 1997 ed.

"Regional Food." Indian Food Reference Guide. www.sanjeevkapoor.com/reference/regional/regionalfood.html

Kanitkar, V. P. (Hemant). *Indian Food and Drink.* New York: The Bookwright Press, 1987.

USING the Rubric for Assessment

Go to page 128 in the **Practice** the Strategy **Notebook!** Use that rubric to assess Maya's paper. Try using the rubric to assess your own writing.

your own EXPOSITORY writing

Science

Put the strategies you practiced in this unit to work to write your own cause-and-effect report, research report, or both! You can:

- develop the writing you did in the Your Own Writing pages of the *Practice the Strategy Notebook*;

- pick an idea below and write something new;

- choose another idea of your own.

Be sure to follow the steps in the writing process. Use the rubrics in this unit to assess your writing.

Cause-and-Effect Report	Research Report
• about no-till farming • about hot springs • about the workings of a car engine • about water conservation • about solar energy or wind energy • about depletion of aquifers	• about the La Brea Tar Pits • about amber jewelry • about dung beetles • about the 1883 Krakatoa volcanic eruption • about early coal mining in America

portfolio

School–Home Connection

Keep a writing portfolio. Think about adding the activities from the *Practice the Strategy Notebook* to your writing portfolio. You may want to take your portfolio home to share.

TEST
writing

A writing test measures how well you can organize your ideas on an assigned topic.

Test Writing

- ☑ starts with a writing prompt.
- ☑ may not let writers use outside sources.
- ☑ may have a time limit.
- ☑ may not allow writers to recopy.

TEST writing

Analyze the Writing Prompt

Every writing test starts with a writing prompt. Most writing prompts have three parts, but the parts are not always labeled. They include the Setup, the Task, and the Scoring Guide.
Read the writing prompt below carefully.

TEST MODEL WRITING

Think about a problem in your school or community that should be fixed.

Explain what the problem is, why it needs to be corrected, and how you would go about fixing it. Be sure your writing

- clearly identifies the topic for your audience early in the paper.
- is well organized. You should include an introduction, body, and conclusion.
- includes details or facts that help readers understand each main idea.
- uses signal words to connect ideas.
- uses the conventions of language and spelling correctly.

This part of the writing prompt gives you the background information you need to get ready to write.

Think about a problem in your school or community that should be fixed.

This part of the writing prompt tells you exactly what you are supposed to write: an explanation of a problem in your school or community with ideas on how to fix it.

Explain what the problem is, why it needs to be corrected, and how you would go about fixing it.

This section tells how your writing will be scored. To do well on the test, you should make sure your writing does everything on the list.

Be sure your writing
- clearly identifies the topic for your audience early in the paper.
- is well organized. You should include an introduction, body, and conclusion.
- includes details or facts that help readers understand each main idea.
- uses signal words to connect ideas.
- uses the conventions of language and spelling correctly.

Using the Scoring Guide

to Study the Model

"Hi. I'm Amber. Like you, I have to take a writing test sometimes. I always pay close attention to the Scoring Guide in the writing prompt.

"Remember the rubrics you saw earlier in this book? Those rubrics helped you work on the areas that are most important in your writing: **Audience, Organization, Elaboration, Clarification,** and **Conventions & Skills**.

"When you take a writing test, you don't always have all the information that's on a rubric. However, you will probably have a Scoring Guide. A Scoring Guide is a lot like a rubric.

"On the next page, you can see what one student wrote in response to the writing prompt on page 228. After you read this explanation, we'll use the Scoring Guide in the writing prompt to see how well she did."

A Place for Us
by Bonnie Campbell

A big problem in our community is that many middle-school students have nowhere to go after school. I would like to explain my solution to this problem.

There are many kids in our town who would like to spend time together after school. I'm not talking about kids who play sports. I'm concerned about a whole group of other kids like me who have nothing to do after school. Our parents don't like us to get together at our homes when no adults are there, so where can we go?

There is no place for us to hang out without getting in trouble. If we go to the diner for a snack, we can't stay there too long. The servers complain that we don't spend enough money to take up the tables. If we go to the library, people complain that we are too noisy. If we get together outside the shops downtown, sometimes adults tell us to move. They say we're blocking the sidewalk.

Now that I've explained the problem, I'd like to explain my solution to it. There is an empty store on Main Street. If we could make this a drop-in center, it would keep students off the street. We could play table tennis and air hockey. There could also be quiet areas for kids to do their home-work. In addition, it would be great if we had a little kitchen or some machines with snacks, too. Another thing I know kids would like would be if we could listen to music there and maybe watch some videos.

This way, kids would not have to go home to empty houses or apart-ments after school. They would not be on the street. Kids with no place to go would not be bored and get into trouble. There could be one or two adults at the center to make sure everyone behaves. We kids could even help out. We could keep the place clean and do other jobs like making snacks. We could help pay for the center by having fund-raisers, like a car wash.

With a special place for kids to go after school, everybody wins! Kids stay busy and have fun, and parents don't have to worry about where they are.

❝ Look at each part of the Scoring Guide. Then look at what Bonnie Campbell wrote. See if you can find examples to show how well her explanation did on each part of the Scoring Guide. **❞**

Scoring Guide

The writer clearly identifies the topic for the audience early in the paper.

Audience

❝ This part of the **Scoring Guide** is about the audience. Let's see. Right in the opening paragraph, Bonnie tells what the problem is. She also says that she has an idea on how to fix it. That's going to be the topic of this explanation. **❞**

A big problem in our community is that many middle-school students have nowhere to go after school. I would like to explain my solution to this problem.

❝ In the rest of her explanation, all the ideas Bonnie included are about her topic: why having no place to go is a problem and how she would fix it. **❞**

The paper is well organized. The writer includes an introduction, body, and conclusion.

Organization

" This part of the **Scoring Guide** is about how Bonnie organized her writing. We just read her introduction. In the body, she explains why having no place to go is a problem. "

There is no place for us to hang out without getting in trouble. If we go to the diner for a snack, we can't stay there too long. The servers complain that we don't spend enough money to take up the tables. If we go to the library, people complain that we are too noisy. . . .

" Then Bonnie goes on to explain how she would fix the problem. Finally, she uses her conclusion to wrap up all her ideas. "

With a special place for kids to go after school, everybody wins! Kids stay busy and have fun, and parents don't have to worry about where they are.

The writer includes details or facts that help readers understand each main idea.

Elaboration

" Bonnie elaborates on her ideas by including details about how kids could help out at the center. These details helped me understand what she meant. "

We kids could even help out. We could keep the place clean and do other jobs like making snacks. We could help pay for the center by having fund-raisers, like a car wash.

The writer uses signal words to connect ideas.

Clarification

❝ Signal words help readers follow a writer's ideas. That's what the clarification step does. Can you find the signal words Bonnie used in this part of her explanation? ❞

There could also be quiet areas for kids to do their homework. In addition, it would be great if we had a little kitchen or some machines with snacks, too. Another thing I know kids would like would be if we could listen to music there and maybe watch some videos.

Scoring Guide

The writer uses the conventions of language and spelling correctly.

Conventions & Skills

❝ As far as I can tell, Bonnie did not make any mistakes in capitalization, punctuation, or sentence completeness. Can you find any below? ❞

Now that I've explained the problem, I'd like to explain my solution to it. There is an empty store on Main Street. If we could make this a drop-in center, it would keep students off the street.

❝ **Now I'm ready to write!**

I will respond to another writing prompt, and you can see how well I do! ❞

Amber

Test Writing Champ

Name:	Amber
Favorite Subject:	science
Favorite Book:	*Steal Away Home* by Lois Ruby
Hobbies:	using my telescope, training dogs
Assignment:	an explanation for a writing test

Prewriting

Gather

Read and analyze the writing prompt. Make sure I understand what I am supposed to do.

"Let's look at a piece of writing I am doing for a test. That will help you work on your own writing test strategies. To begin, study the writing prompt carefully. It will probably have three parts, but the parts won't be labeled for you. You need to find the Setup, Task, and **Scoring Guide** yourself.

"Of course, the first thing writers do when they write is gather information. When you write to take a test, you start gathering information from the writing prompt. That's why it's important to read the writing prompt carefully. You've got to analyze it and make sure you know exactly what you're supposed to do.

"Here's the writing prompt I have.

Setup — Suppose you have an opportunity to travel on a space shuttle.

Task — Write an essay explaining why you would or would not want to go on a space shuttle. Be sure your writing

Scoring Guide
- clearly identifies the topic for your audience early in the paper.
- is well organized. You should include an introduction, body, and conclusion.
- includes details or facts that help readers understand each main idea.
- uses signal words to connect ideas.
- uses the conventions of language and spelling correctly.

> Before I do anything else, I take five minutes to really study the writing prompt. I follow these steps so I know what to do.

1 Read all three parts of the writing prompt carefully.

> All right, I found the **Setup,** the **Task,** and the **Scoring Guide**.

2 Circle key words in the Task that tell what kind of writing I need to do and who my audience is.

> I circled the words **an opportunity to travel on a space shuttle**. That's the topic of my writing. I also circled the words **an essay explaining why** because that tells me the kind of writing I will be doing: an explanation. The prompt doesn't identify my audience, so I'll write for my teacher. Of course, first I have to decide whether I want to take a ride on a shuttle!

3 Make sure I know how I'll be graded.

> The **Scoring Guide** tells what I should include to get a good score. I need to pay close attention to that!

4 Say what I need to do in my own words.

> Here's what I'm supposed to do: tell whether or not I want to take a ride on a space shuttle and explain why.

Go to page 130 in the **Practice the Strategy Notebook!**

Prewriting

Organize   Plan my time.

"Prewriting is a little different when you take a test. You need to keep an eye on the clock. Think about how much time you have and divide the time up into the different parts of the writing process. If the test takes an hour, here's how I might organize my time."

Analyze the prompt
5 minutes

Edit
5 minutes

Prewrite
15 minutes

Revise
10 minutes

Draft
25 minutes

Prewriting
Gather & Organize

Choose a graphic organizer. Use it to organize my ideas.

"I don't have much time, so I'll gather ideas and organize them at the same time. First, I'll choose a useful graphic organizer. I'm writing an explanation, so a spider map will help me remember the important ideas I want to include. The map will help me keep track of main ideas and details. Some of the information comes right out of the Setup and Task parts of the writing prompt.

"I've already decided I really would like to fly on a shuttle. I'll write that in the center circle of my spider map. Now I'll identify the reasons why and write the main ones on each leg. If you need more information about using a spider map, look in Unit 2 on page 87."

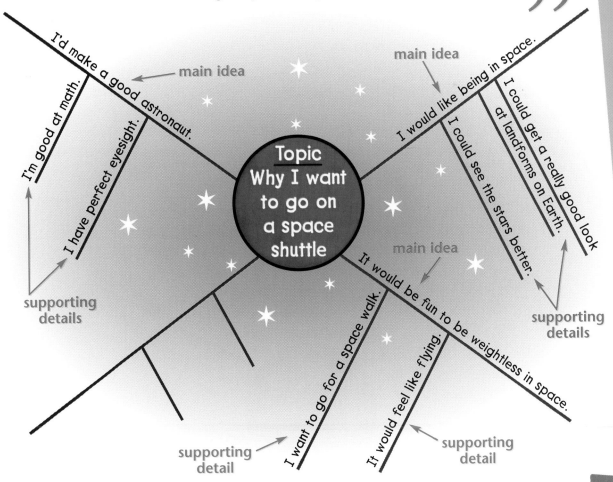

main idea

main idea

main idea

I'd make a good astronaut.

I'm good at math.

I have perfect eyesight.

I would like being in space.

I could get a really good look at landforms on Earth.

I could see the stars better.

Topic
Why I want to go on a space shuttle

It would be fun to be weightless in space.

I want to go for a space walk.

It would feel like flying.

supporting details

supporting details

supporting detail

supporting detail

Prewriting

Organize
Check my graphic organizer against the Scoring Guide.

> In a test, you don't always get much time to revise. That makes prewriting more important than ever! Even before I write, I'll check my spider map against the **Scoring Guide** in the writing prompt. My paper should do everything that's listed in the **Scoring Guide**.

 Be sure your writing clearly identifies the topic for your audience early in the paper.

> I'm going to write about why I'd like to travel on a space shuttle. That's the topic I wrote in the center of my spider map.

Topic
Why I want to go on a space shuttle

 Be sure your writing is well organized. You should include an introduction, body, and conclusion.

> I'll use the topic in the center of my spider map to write an introduction. That's where I'll explain that I do want to go on a shuttle. I'll use the main ideas from the legs of my spider map in the body of my explanation. That's where I'll explain the reasons for my decision.
>
> "Then I'll restate my decision and wrap things up in my conclusion.

Topic
Why I want to go on a space shuttle

I would like being in space.

Be sure your writing includes details or facts that help readers understand each main idea.

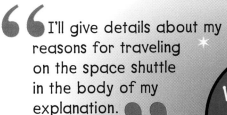

Topic
Why I want to go on a space shuttle

I would like being in space.

I could get a really good look at landforms on Earth.

I could see the stars better.

It would be fun to be weightless in space.

I want to go for a space walk.

It would feel like flying.

" I'll give details about my reasons for traveling on the space shuttle in the body of my explanation. "

Be sure your writing uses signal words to connect ideas.

" As I write, I'll remember to use signal words like **most important** and **finally**. "

Be sure your writing uses the conventions of language and spelling correctly.

" For my last step, I'll check my grammar, punctuation, capitalization, and spelling. "

Go to page 131 in the **Practice** the Strategy **Notebook!**

Drafting

Write

Use my spider map to write an explanation with a good introduction, body, and conclusion.

> After I checked my spider map one more time, here's what I wrote. I left room to make corrections.

The Sky's the Limit!
by Amber

[DRAFT]

introduction

If I ever had an opportunity to go on the space shuttle, ~~I think~~ I would jump at the chance. Actually, maybe I should say I would fly at the chance! There are several reasons why I think this would be the experience of a lifetime.

First of all, I think I would make a good astronaut. ~~Because~~ I like all of the rides at amusement parks, even the ones where you turn upside down. I'm also good in math, and I have ~~really good~~ perfect eyesight, so those are two more things in my favor.

body

I would be fascinated by the whole experience of being in space. I love looking at the stars from here on Earth. ~~The stars look sort of~~ I can only imagine how much better stargazing would be up in the sky. The other astronauts and me could look down at Earth when we got tired of stargazing. I've read that you can see Rivers, Mountains, and other landforms from space.

I think that moving around without gravity wood be just about like flying. My greatest dream is to go for a space walk. Walking in space would be just about the best thing I can imagine. Some people might be afraid of floating into space forever I don't think that would be a problem. The people who designed the space shuttle and all of it's equipment is very careful about everything they do.

I know that ~~mon~~ many people would not enjoy being cooped up in an area as small as the shuttle with other people. Eating and drinking food from tubes. Those things wouldn't bother me, though. Instead, being in space would make me really appreciate what I have here on earth.

With my skills my interest in space, and my lack of fear, I think I would be a good person to travel in a shuttle. Now, wear can I sign up?

body

conclusion

" Remember, you may not get a chance to recopy your paper in a writing test. Try to be neat when you write. "

Go to page 132 in the **Practice** the Strategy **Notebook!**

Revising

Elaborate

Check what I have written against the Scoring Guide. Add any missing facts or details.

> In a test, I can't read my paper to a partner, so I'll read it to myself. I'll keep the **Scoring Guide** in mind and see if anything is missing.
>
> "The **Scoring Guide** says that I need to include details or facts that help readers understand each main idea. I think I should add more details about why I would be a good astronaut.

READ TO MYSELF

[DRAFT]

First of all, I think I would make a good astronaut.

~~Because~~ I like all of the rides at amusement parks, even the ones where you turn upside down, so all of the motion wouldn't bother me. I'm also good in math, and I have ~~really good~~ perfect eyesight, so those are two more things in my favor. I like working on a team with other people. A knack for helping others get along. In a place like the space shuttle, if you don't have good teamwork, you could be in serious trouble.

added details

Go to page 134 in the **Practice** the Strategy **Notebook!**

Revising

Clarify

Check what I have written against the Scoring Guide. Make sure I have used signal words so that everything is clear.

> ❝I'll read my paper again and see if any parts could be clearer. The **Scoring Guide** says that I should use signal words to connect ideas. I see some places where I can add signal words that will make my writing clearer.❞

READ TO MYSELF

signal words

→ Second,
　 ∧I would be fascinated by the whole experience of being in space.
I love looking at the stars from here on Earth. ~~The stars look sort~~ _, so_

~~of~~ I can only imagine how much better stargazing would be up in the
What's more,
　 sky.∧The other astronauts and me could look down at Earth when
　　　　　　　　　　　　In fact,
we got tired of stargazing.∧I've read that you can see Rivers,

Mountains, and other landforms from space.

　 I think that moving around without gravity wood be just ~~about~~ like

flying. My greatest dream∧is to go for a space walk. Walking in
　　　　　　　　　　, however,

space would be just about the best thing I can imagine.

signal words

Go to page 135 in the **Practice** the Strategy **Notebook!**

Editing

Proofread

Check that I have used correct grammar, capitalization, punctuation, and spelling.

"The **Scoring Guide** says to use correct grammar, capitalization, punctuation, and spelling. I always leave plenty of time to check for errors in these important areas.

"We've used a checklist like the one below so often that I almost have it memorized. On the next page, you can see the errors I found and fixed. It's a good thing I proofread my test!"

Proofreading Checklist

- ☑ Do all the sentences have a subject and verb?
- ☑ Do the subjects and verbs agree?
- ☑ Have compound sentences been joined with a comma and a conjunction or with a semicolon?
- ☑ Do all proper nouns, proper adjectives, and related words begin with a capital letter?
- ☑ Have subject and object pronouns been used correctly?
- ☑ Does each pronoun have a clear antecedent and agree with its antecedent?
- ☑ Are appositives used correctly?
- ☑ Are apostrophes used correctly in possessive nouns and contractions?
- ☑ Are the correct forms of homophones used?
- ☑ Are all words spelled correctly?

Extra Practice
See **Review** (pages CS 22–CS 23) in the back of this book.

[DRAFT]

The Sky's the Limit
by Amber

    If I ever had an opportunity to go on the space shuttle, ~~I think~~ I would jump at the chance. Actually, maybe I should say I would fly at the chance! There are several reasons why I think this would be the experience of a lifetime.

    First of all, I think I would make a good astronaut. ~~Because~~ I like all of the rides at amusement parks, even the ones where you turn upside down. , so all of the motion wouldn't bother me I'm also good in math, and I have ~~really good~~ perfect eyesight, so those are two more things in my favor. I like working on a team with other people, and I have a knack for helping others get along. In a place like the space shuttle, if you don't have good teamwork, you could be in serious trouble.

Second,
∧I would be fascinated by the whole experience of being in space.

I love looking at the stars from here on Earth. ~~The stars look sort of~~
                                              , so
I can only imagine how much better stargazing would be up in the
What's more,   ∧I
sky. ∧The other astronauts and ~~me~~ could look down at Earth when we
                    In fact,
got tired of stargazing. I've read that you can see Rivers, Mountains,

and other landforms from space.

I think that moving around without gravity ~~wood~~ be just ~~about~~ like
                                        would
                    , however,
flying. My greatest dream∧is to go for a space walk. Walking in

space would be just about the best thing I can imagine. Some people
                                          , but
might be afraid of floating into space forever∧I don't think that

would be a problem. The people who designed the space shuttle
                                    are
and all of it's equipment ~~is~~∧very careful about everything they do.

I know that ~~mon~~ many people would not enjoy being cooped up in

an area as small as the shuttle with other people. Eating and drink-

ing food from tubes. Those things wouldn't bother me, though.

Instead, being in space would make me really appreciate what I

have here on earth.

With my skills, my interest in space, and my lack of fear, I think I
                                                    where
would be a good person to travel in a shuttle. Now, ~~wear~~∧can I

sign up?

                                the Strategy
Go to page 136 in the **Practice**∧**Notebook!**

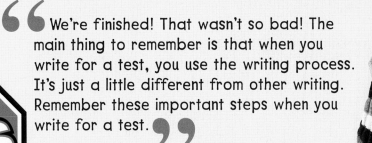

We're finished! That wasn't so bad! The main thing to remember is that when you write for a test, you use the writing process. It's just a little different from other writing. Remember these important steps when you write for a test.

1. **Analyze the writing prompt before you start to write.**
   Most writing prompts have three parts: the Setup, the Task, and the Scoring Guide. The three parts are not labeled for you. You need to figure them out for yourself.

2. **Make sure you understand the task before you start to write. Remember to**
   - read all three parts of the writing prompt carefully.
   - circle key words in the Task part of the writing prompt that tell what kind of writing you need to do and who your audience is. If you do not know who the audience is, write for your teacher.
   - make sure you know how you will be graded.
   - say what you need to do in your own words.

3. **Keep an eye on the clock.**
   Decide how much time you're going to spend on each part of the writing process and try to stick to it. Do not spend so much time on prewriting that you do not have any time left to write!

4. **Reread your writing. Check it against the Scoring Guide at least twice.**
   Remember the rubrics we've used all year? If you keep them in mind, you will probably write better. A Scoring Guide on a writing test is like a rubric. It can help you keep what's important in mind.

5. **Plan, plan, plan!**
   You do not get as much time to revise during a test, so planning is more important than ever.

6. **Write neatly.**
   Remember, if the people who score your test cannot read your writing, it does not matter how good your paper is!

your own TEST writing

Expository

Put the strategies you practiced in this unit to work. Use the writing prompt below or come up with your own idea. Then take your own expository writing test. Pretend this is a real test and give yourself one hour to complete all of the steps. Use the Scoring Guide below to evaluate your paper.

Think about an invention or a product that you wish existed today. Tell about this idea. Explain how it would work or be used and how it would improve the lives of those who use it. Be sure your writing

- clearly identifies the topic for your audience early in the paper.

- is well organized. You should include an introduction, body, and conclusion.

- includes details or facts that help readers understand each main idea.

- uses signal words to connect ideas.

- uses the conventions of language and spelling correctly.

portfolio

School–Home Connection

Keep a writing portfolio. Think about adding the activities from the *Practice the Strategy Notebook* to your writing portfolio. You may want to take your portfolio home to share.

Extra Practice

Conventions & SKiLLS

The activities on the following pages provide additional practice in the grammar, usage, and mechanics skills you worked with throughout this book. Use the activities to get extra practice in these skills. Complete each activity on a separate sheet of paper.

Table of Contents

A **sentence** is a group of words that tells a complete thought. Every sentence must have a **subject** and a **verb**. A sentence that is missing a subject or a verb is an incomplete sentence, or a **fragment**.

A simple sentence tells one complete thought. Two simple sentences with related ideas can be joined to form a **compound sentence**. When two simple sentences are joined incorrectly, they form a **run-on sentence**.

ReView the Rule

A sentence that is missing a subject or a verb is called a **fragment.**

Fragment: Looked forward to the rodeo. (subject missing)

Fragment: A clown on the fence. (verb missing)

When you join two sentences as a **compound sentence,** put a comma followed by a conjunction between them. You can also join them with a semicolon. Sentences that are not joined correctly are called **run-ons.**

Joined correctly: Rodeo clowns look funny, but they take their work seriously.

Joined correctly: Rodeo clowns look funny; they take their work seriously.

Run-on: Rodeo clowns look funny, they take their work seriously.

Practice

Decide whether the sentence fragments below need a subject or a verb. Then write the complete sentences on a separate piece of paper.

1. Gripping the reins tightly.
2. Bulls with names like Turbo and Jackhammer.
3. Streaked from the chute like a shot from a cannon.
4. The glory of riding the wildest.
5. A whirlwind of kicks and bucks.

On your paper, join these pairs of simple sentences, forming compound sentences. You may need to add or delete some words when you rewrite. Punctuate your sentences correctly.

6. The announcer named the winners. The crowd cheered for each one.

7. Some people protest the use of animals in rodeos. Rodeo animals are well treated.

8. Chaps protect a cowboy's legs. Gloves protect his hands.

9. Bronc riders earn points for form and control. Broncs earn points for bucking.

10. I thought I had seen the best ride ever. Then I saw a better one!

11. The first buck tosses you one way. The second one flings you the other way.

12. We finished our chores. Then we headed for the rodeo.

13. I picked out a souvenir hat. Dad chose cuff links shaped like horseshoes.

14. A bronc rider can get off a horse by himself. He can get help from a pickup man.

15. Some women ride in rough stock events. Most are barrel racers.

Read this paragraph about Buffalo Bill's Wild West Show. Look for fragments and run-ons. Write the paragraph correctly on your paper.

> "Buffalo Bill" Cody's Wild West Show spread the myth of the West for more than 30 years. The show began in 1882. Reenactments of stagecoach robberies and buffalo hunts. Cody died in 1917, his last words were said to be, "Let my show go on!" Montie Montana, Jr., has brought Buffalo Bill's Wild West Show back to life and I think Buffalo Bill would have approved.

A **quotation** is the exact words of a speaker or a writer. Quotations can add interest to nearly every piece of writing. However, quotations must be punctuated correctly.

ReView the Rule

Use quotation marks at the beginning and end of a quotation. Use a comma to separate the speaker's words from the rest of the sentence. If a quotation is a complete sentence, begin it with a capital letter. Add the correct end punctuation before the last quotation mark.

Examples: "Will people believe us?" asked Newell.

Hull said, "Of course they will!"

Practice

Now let's use what you learned. On a separate piece of paper, number from 1.–15. Then write the sentences below, correcting the capitalization and punctuation of the quotations.

1. To the people at the quarry, Hull said The stone is for a patriotic statue.

2. One article said, Hull was the model for the giant's face.

3. Newell asked "Should I dig up the giant myself or have it dug up by others."

4. What is it? Who carved it? How old is it? Why was it buried? everyone asked.

5. A politician said It has the mark of ages stamped upon it.

6. "It's humbug! declared a well-known paleontologist.

7. People began telling each other, The giant is a Goliath"!

8. "It is positively absurd to consider this a fossil man. said geologist J. F. Boynton.

9. Boynton wrote visitors hardly spoke above a whisper.

10. The stonecutters said we'll keep quiet. Don't worry!

11. Historians say "Hull was a cheat and a scoundrel.

12. One newspaper reported "Hull was a Dr. Frankenstein who created a monster."

13. Hull said I was merely playing a practical joke on the public.

14. I knew it! shouted the skeptics when Hull admitted the hoax.

15. A reporter wrote the giant was both a mystery and a success.

The Cardiff Giant hoax occurred during the Victorian Age. On your paper, rewrite this paragraph about the Victorian Age. Correct any mistakes in the punctuation of the quotations.

The Victorian Age might have been called the Alexandrina Age. Queen Victoria was christened Alexandrina Victoria, but she was always called Victoria. People preferred the name Victoria, historians wrote.

Victoria's governess said "Victoria first learned of her future role as the British ruler during a history lesson when she was 10 years old.

"In response to this news, Victoria said I will be good.

Queen Victoria ascended to the throne in 1837 and moved into Buckingham Palace. She said "I never had a room all to myself before"!

 Homophones

Homophones are words that are pronounced the same but have different spellings and meanings.

ReView the Rule

Here are some examples of homophones and their meanings. Make sure you are using the correct word.

its – possessive pronoun meaning "belonging to it"
it's – contraction of *it is* or *it has*

there – adverb meaning "in that place"
their – possessive pronoun meaning "belonging to them"
they're – contraction of *they are*

two – number
to – word meaning "toward"; also used with a verb (*to run, to sing*)
too – word meaning "also" or "more than enough"

your – possessive pronoun meaning "belonging to you"
you're – contraction of *you are*

whose – possessive pronoun meaning "belonging to someone"
who's – contraction of *who is* or *who has*

Practice

Number your paper 1.–10. For each sentence below, write the correct word.

1. Three chords and a simple pattern give the blues (its/it's) unique form.

2. (It's/Its) one of the oldest forms of American music.

3. (There/Their/They're) are several views about the origins of the blues.

4. These songs are called the blues because (there/their/they're) often sad.

5. At first, only people in the South sang or listened (two/to/too) the blues.

6. By the 1920s, people in the North were enjoying the blues, (two/to/too).

7. (Two/To/Too) forms of music—jazz and blues—are often combined.

8. Many of (your/you're) favorite country and rock songs are based on the blues.

9. T-Bone Walker was a blues guitarist (whose/who's) style made the electric guitar popular.

10. (Whose/Who's) going to deny that Elvis Presley was inspired by the blues?

Read this paragraph from a letter about blues singer Koko Taylor. Write the paragraph on your paper, correcting any mistakes in word use.

> In you're music magazine, you wrote that the blues is sad music. Some of it is sad, but some is happy, two. When you listen to Koko Taylor, whose considered one of the best female blues artists, you want to get up and dance. Their is nothing more joyful than her foot-stomping blues. Your not going to be sorry if you let your readers know about Koko, and there not going too be sad.

Subject-Verb Agreement

Every sentence must have a subject and a verb. A **singular subject** requires a **singular verb,** and a **plural subject** requires a **plural verb**. In many sentences, a prepositional phrase comes between the subject and the verb. A prepositional phrase is a group of words that begins with a preposition and ends with an object.

ReView the Rule

Do not mistake the object of the preposition for the subject of the sentence. The verb in every sentence must match its subject, not the object of the preposition (op).

> **Incorrect:** All the colonies in New England was separate.
>
> **Correct:** All the colonies in New England were separate.
>
> **Incorrect:** One of the patriots were named Joseph Wadsworth.
>
> **Correct:** One of the patriots was named Joseph Wadsworth.

Practice

Now let's put to use what you have learned. Number your paper 1.–15. and write the correct verb form for each sentence.

1. Connecticut (is/are/am) one of six New England states.

2. Maine (was/were) the last New England colony to become a state.

3. The U.S. Mint (is/are/am) issuing state quarters between 1999 and 2008.

4. The first state quarter for New England (was/were) for Connecticut.

5. Many people in this country (collect/collects) state quarters.

6. Usually, a coin (gain/gains) in value over time.

7. The value of coins (change/changes), depending on supply and demand.

8. Six states across the nation (has/have) chosen the oak as their state tree.

9. Seventeen of the states (has/have) selected the pine as their state tree.

10. The branches of an oak (spread/spreads) out like an umbrella.

11. Wood from oak trees (make/makes) sturdy furniture.

12. Large forests (was/were) common in New England during the colonial period.

13. Trees in older parts of town (is/are/am) usually older than those in new sections.

14. The planting of trees (prevent/prevents) soil erosion.

15. A row of trees beside a building (serve/serves) as a windbreak.

Read this paragraph from a summary. Write the paragraph on your paper, correcting any errors in subject-verb agreement.

White oaks grow on dry to moist sites. The acorns from this tree is important to both people and wildlife. Long ago, Native Americans made flour from these acorns. Many kinds of wildlife in the forest depends on the acorns for food. The wood from white oaks are used to make hardwood floors and boats. The USS Constitution was called "Old Ironsides," but most of this ship were made from white oak.

Complex Sentences

A **complex sentence** contains an independent clause and a dependent clause. An **independent clause** has a subject and a verb. It is also a simple sentence. A **dependent clause** has a subject and a verb but does not make sense by itself. It is one kind of **sentence fragment**. Dependent clauses begin with **subordinating conjunctions** such as *although, because, if, as, so, before,* or *when.*

ReView the Rule

A dependent clause should be combined with an independent clause. That way, you create a complex sentence and avoid using sentence fragments.

Example:

Independent clause:

You will make wise decisions.

Dependent clause (sentence fragment):

If you think carefully.

Dependent clause + independent clause = complex sentence:

If you think carefully, you will make wise decisions.

Practice

Number your paper 1.–5. Read each group of words and write **CX** if it is a complex sentence or **F** (fragment) if it is a dependent clause.

1. Although Lois Lowry has written many books, *Number the Stars* was her first to win the Newbery Award.

2. When Lowry learned about the rescue of Jews in Denmark during World War II.

3. After the Nazis began to threaten the Danish Jews, the Danish Resistance smuggled nearly 7,000 Jews to safety.

4. If you were a Jew in Denmark during the early 1940s.

5. A resistance is a secret organization because it works against a government.

Now number your paper 6.–12. Match each dependent clause on the left with an independent clause on the right to form a complex sentence. Write the complex sentence on your paper.

6. When it became clear that the war was going to involve many nations,

7. Because Sweden was a neutral country and near Denmark,

8. Although all countries had the right to stay neutral,

9. When she wrote *Good Night, Maman* in 1999,

10. Although their stories have been turned into fiction,

11. As Mazer tried to get the correct balance of history and fiction,

12. When Mazer was growing up near Oswego, New York,

some people thought Sweden should have taken sides in the war.

the refugee camp was located near her home.

most Danish Jews were taken to Sweden.

she rewrote the book four times.

Sweden announced its neutrality in the war.

the book is based on real refugees who came to America during World War II.

Norma Fox Mazer was already a well-known author.

Read this paragraph from a book review. Write the paragraph on your paper, correcting any errors in using dependent clauses as sentences.

> Although death is a controversial topic. Most young-adult authors have tackled it in their books. Because cancer is a common terminal illness. Many books deal with death of a family member by cancer. These include <u>After the Rain</u> by Norma Fox Mazer and <u>A Summer to Die</u> by Lois Lowry. Death is tragic. So the authors handle it gently.

Pronouns and Antecedents

A **pronoun** is a word that takes the place of a noun. An **antecedent** is the noun or phrase that the pronoun refers to.

A pronoun must agree with its antecedent in two ways:

- The pronoun must be singular if its antecedent is singular. The pronoun must be plural if its antecedent is plural.

- The pronoun must be female if its antecedent is female—or male if its antecedent is male.

Review the Rule

When you use a pronoun, make sure that its antecedent is clear. Also, make sure that the pronoun agrees with its antecedent.

Unclear antecedent:
Mark's friend is named Jamal. **He** lives down the street. (It is unclear whether *He* refers to *Mark* or *Jamal*.)

Clearer:
Mark's friend Jamal lives down the street. (Sometimes the best way to correct an unclear antecedent is not to use a pronoun at all!)

Pronouns that agree:
Stereotyping might lead a girl to choose **her** friends based on the clothes **they** wear. (*Her* is singular and female, so it agrees with its singular antecedent, *girl. They* is plural and agrees with its plural antecedent, *friends.*)

Practice

For sentences 1.–5., identify the antecedent for the underlined pronoun. Write the antecedent on a separate sheet of paper.

1. Stereotyping is a part of our culture. <u>It</u> is something we should try to change.

2. Stereotyping occurs when people are grouped together. Perhaps <u>they</u> are grouped because they all play football or chess.

3. We make poor judgments when we stereotype individuals. We do not respect <u>them</u>.

4. Stereotypes can be positive or negative, but <u>they</u> are almost always unfair.

5. Victims of stereotyping often do not know what to do about <u>it</u>.

For sentences 6.–10., choose the correct pronoun and write it on your paper. Sometimes you will write the pronoun and its verb.

6. People often stereotype others based on the clothing (he is/she is/they are) wearing.

7. When we see a man in shabby clothing, we may assume that (he is/they are) homeless.

8. In fact, he may just not care what others think of (him/her/them).

9. When we see girls smoking cigarettes, we might assume that (she doesn't/they don't) care about their health.

10. Perhaps those girls have heard about the hazards of smoking but do not believe (it is/they are) real.

On your paper, rewrite this paragraph from a persuasive essay. Correct any errors in matching pronoun antecedents or using unclear antecedents.

> Some people think teenagers are very likely to use stereotypes to choose their friends. However, they are wrong. Teenagers are not more likely to use it than other groups of people. People of any age may stereotype others, perhaps based on his appearance. Many people tend to choose friends who look like you. They must try to keep an open mind when they choose your friends.

An **appositive** is a word or phrase that follows a noun and helps identify or describe it.

ReView the Rule

Appositives follow nouns and add more information about the nouns. They are usually separated from the rest of the sentence by commas.

Examples: Dolly, **my cat,** came to our house as a stray.

My neighbor's dogs, **two boxers,** bark at night.

Practice

Now let's put to use what you have learned. Number your paper 1.–15. For the first group of sentences below, write the noun and the appositive that follows it on your paper.

1. Here are some tips, or guidelines, for getting good photographs of your pets.

2. The first tip, and the most important one, is to study your pet.

3. Find your pet's favorite spot, the place where it likes to spend most of its time.

4. For example, Bubba, my shaggy sheepdog, likes to hang out on the braided rug in the den.

5. Observe your pet's typical behavior, what he or she does every day.

6. My cat lounges by the "pool," her water bowl, when it's hot.

7. As you take the picture, be prepared for sudden movement, a turning head or a twitching ear.

8. Use a fast shutter speed, at least 1/125 or 1/250, to prevent blurring.

9. Point of view, the perspective of your photo, is also important.

10. Use treats, tools of the pet photographer's trade, to get your pet's attention.

In this group of sentences, notice the underlined nouns or pronouns. On your paper, write an appositive that you could use for each underlined word.

11. Our <u>neighbor</u>, _____, likes to take pictures of his dog.

12. His best <u>picture</u>, _____, won a prize last year.

13. Our neighbor's <u>daughter</u>, _____, takes the dog for walks.

14. They usually head for their favorite <u>spot</u>, _____.

15. Our neighbor has many pictures of the two of <u>them</u>, _____, at the park.

Read this paragraph from a descriptive essay about two cats. Write the paragraph on your paper, correcting any errors in appositives.

I have two tiger cats or tabbies. A tabby is a striped shorthair a breed of cat. Hansel, the male cat is a butterscotch tabby with lemon-drop eyes. His sister Gretel is a chocolate-cinnamon tabby. Hansel and Gretel are named for the storybook characters the ones who are abandoned in the woods. My cats look like they live in the candy house because they are so chubby and sweet.

Conventions & Skills — Apostrophes

Apostrophes

Apostrophes are used in possessive nouns and contractions. A **possessive noun** shows ownership. A **contraction** is a word formed from two words, such as *I'm* (*I am*) and *didn't* (*did not*).

ReView the Rule

- To form the **possessive** of a singular noun, add an apostrophe and *s*.
  Example: My brother**'s** hobby is racing slot cars.

- To form the **possessive** of a plural noun that ends in *s*, just add an apostrophe.
  Example: He joined a slot car racers**'** club.

- To form the **possessive** of a plural noun that does not end in *s*, add an apostrophe and *s*.
  Example: The club has a large men**'s** group and a small women**'s** group.

- To form a **contraction,** use an apostrophe to replace dropped letters.
  Example: They**'**re crazy about this hobby.

Practice

Now let's use what you have learned. Number a separate sheet of paper 1.–15. Read this first group of sentences, choose the correct form in parentheses, and write it on your paper.

1. One (dictionary's/dictionarys') definition says a slot car is "an electric toy racing car with a pin underneath that fits into a groove on a track."

2. The (car's/cars') bodies are made of plastic or metal.

3. A slot (car's/cars') power is transmitted through steel rails in the track.

4. My (dad's/dads') oldest track layout is from the 1960s.

5. (It's/Its') only a two-lane plastic track that snaps together.

6. Lately, (he's/hes') been racing on a track called the Blue King.

7. The Blue (King's/Kings') track has eight lanes.

8. My (mom's/moms') brother, Uncle Jake, bought the track at an auction last year.

Now read this group of sentences. On your paper, write the possessive form or the contraction that would replace the boldfaced words.

9. Uncle Jake **did not** know why he bought the Blue King.

10. He **was not** even a slot car racer.

11. Now, of course, he **cannot** believe how much fun it is.

12. **We have** been racing together every Saturday ever since.

13. The sport **is not** just enjoyed by the men in our family.

14. Slot car racing is a **sport for women,** too.

15. **The car belonging to my sister** won a prize.

Read this paragraph from an observation report on a science experiment. Rewrite it on a separate sheet of paper, correcting any errors in the use of apostrophes.

Taylor, LaShawn, and I stood on the bleachers top row. "Are you ready?" I asked. "Wer'e ready," they answered. At the count of three, we dropped our parachutes, which were each carrying an egg. Taylors' 5-inch parachute was the first to hit the ground. Splat! The eggs' yellow innards oozed out but didnt spread far. My 10-inch parachute was next to hit the ground, followed by LaShawns 15-inch parachute.

Subject and Object Pronouns

A **pronoun** can replace a noun naming a person, place, thing, or idea.

ReView the Rule

- A **subject pronoun** takes the place of the subject in a sentence.

  Example: She lives near Hoover Dam.

- An **object pronoun** replaces the object of a verb or a preposition.

  Example: The dam helps **them** irrigate their fields.

- Use *who* as a subject pronoun. Use *whom* as an object pronoun.

  Examples: Herbert Hoover, **who** was president when the dam construction was approved, made a speech. He talked to farmers for **whom** the dam would make a huge difference. (*Who* is the subject of the verb *was. Whom* is the object of the preposition *for.*)

Practice

Number a separate sheet of paper 1.–15. Choose the correct pronoun for each sentence and write it on your paper. Add **S** if you chose a subject pronoun or **O** if you chose an object pronoun.

1. People (who/whom) live in the desert value water.

2. (I/me) grew up in the Mojave Desert in Nevada.

3. Hoover Dam was built near (us/we) in the early 1930s.

4. For (who/whom) was Hoover Dam built?

5. It was built for all of (we/us) in the Southwest.

6. (Who/Whom) can name the river controlled by the Hoover Dam?

7. People (who/whom) live in the area know it's the Colorado River.

8. (They/Them) may not know that this river carved the Grand Canyon.

9. Hoover Dam supplies hydroelectric power to (we/us) and several other states.

10. (We/Us) also receive water for irrigation and drinking.

11. My grandfather, from (who/whom) I learned about the dam, helped build it.

12. Pioneers (who/whom) settled in the Southwest tried to live near the Colorado River.

13. (Who/Whom) could adapt to a river that flooded in spring and dried up in fall?

14. The people (who/whom) the river affected most needed help.

15. Most people (who/whom) lived near the river wanted the dam to be built.

Apply

Read this paragraph from a cause-and-effect report on the Hoover Dam. Write the paragraph on a separate sheet of paper, correcting any errors in the use of pronouns.

Herbert Hoover was secretary of commerce during the 1920s. During that time, he supervised relief for people whom had been flooded out of their homes by the Mississippi River. Because of his efforts, him was called "The Great Humanitarian." It was Hoover whom urged the building of a huge dam to control the Colorado River. The dam was named for Hoover, whom was president when construction was approved.

A common noun names a person, place, thing, or idea. A **proper noun** names a specific person, place, thing, or idea. **Proper adjectives** are formed from proper nouns.

ReView the Rule

1. Capitalize **proper nouns**.

    Example: My family immigrated to the **United States** from **India**.

2. Capitalize **proper adjectives**.

    Example: Have you ever tasted **Indian** food?

3. Capitalize **titles of respect** when they are used before a person's name.

    Example: Mr. Raj Chopra gave a presentation to our class.

4. Capitalize **proper abbreviations** (words in addresses such as *street* and *avenue*, days, months, and parts of business names in informal notes). End the abbreviations with a period.

    Example: Sakthi's address is 247 Fourteenth **St.**

5. Capitalize an **initial** when it replaces the name of a person or place. Follow the initial with a period.

    Example: Our new neighbor's name is **P. R.** Phalke.

Practice

Number a separate sheet of paper 1.–15. Read each sentence below. Find the error or errors in using proper nouns or proper adjectives and write that part of the sentence correctly on your paper. Add the number of the rule you followed.

1. The indian film industry is over 100 years old.

2. The French Lumière brothers showed six short silent films at a bombay hotel in 1886.

3. Shortly afterwards, Hiralal Sen and H S. Bhatavdekar started making films.

4. india's first talkie, *Alam Ara,* was released in march 1931.

5. Imperial Film Co was the producer of that film.

6. Early talkies were often produced in hindi to reach a wide audience.

7. Others were produced in regional languages, such as marathi.

8. India's famous director, satyajit Ray, gained international recognition.

9. Ray earned an oscar for lifetime achievement in 1995.

10. In the 1960s, the film star Shammi Kapoor became an indian Elvis.

11. Indian movies of the 1970s were action oriented, like many american movies.

12. In 1988, Shaji n. Karun's movie *Piravi* won numerous awards.

13. Musical love stories in the late 1980s included movies such as *Mr India.*

14. India's film industry today is known as bollywood.

15. The International Indian Film Festival is organized by an office at 17 Infantary Rd in Bangalore, India.

Read these paragraphs from a research report on Asian Indians in the United States. Rewrite it on your paper, correcting any errors in the use of proper nouns or proper adjectives.

The number of asian Indians in the United states has doubled in the last 10 years, according to the US. Census bureau. In 2000, 1.7 million people in the US identified themselves as Asian indians or indian Americans.

Mr P Khandhar, a census coordinator, said, "One obvious factor for the growth in the Indian american community is the importing of the hi-tech workers." Mr Khandhar added, "If you look at places like New Jersey and New York city, you are seeing that more Indian Americans specifically are getting involved in politics."

Proofreading Checklist

☑ Do all the sentences have a subject and verb?

☑ Do the subjects and verbs agree?

☑ Have compound sentences been joined with a comma and a conjunction or with a semicolon?

☑ Do all proper nouns, proper adjectives, and related words begin with a capital letter?

☑ Have subject and object pronouns been used correctly?

☑ Does each pronoun have a clear antecedent and agree with its antecedent?

☑ Are appositives used correctly?

☑ Are apostrophes used correctly in possessive nouns and contractions?

☑ Are the correct forms of homophones used?

☑ Are all words spelled correctly?

Practice

Number your paper 1.–15. If a sentence has no errors, write **Correct**. If a sentence has one or more errors, rewrite it, correcting the errors. Use the checklist above.

1. The first space vehicle was shaped like a rocket but it also had wings, a rudder, and wheels.

2. This unusual rocket plane, the X-15 first flew in september 1959.

3. The X-15, however, could do none of the things later spacecraft accomplished.

4. Josh and me watched John Glenn orbit Earth in 1962.

5. It took nearly five hours for Glenns mercury capsule to complete it's three orbits.

6. Gemini 6 and Gemini 7 completed the first rendezvous in space, Gemini 7 spent a record 330 hours and 35 minutes in space.

7. The Apollo flights into space is the ones most people remember.

8. A TV bulletin told my friends and I about a terrible accident at the space center.

9. Three Apollo astronauts were killed when there module caught fire.

10. However, the Apollo program continued and to years later this spacecraft landed on the moon.

11. Alan Shepard, whom piloted the first Mercury flight, also rode Apollo to the moon.

12. The space shuttle program during the 1970s.

13. The test flights of the shuttles went well and soon it was carrying payloads into space.

14. Then one shuttle, the Challenger exploded.

15. Many improvements were made in the shuttles design as a result, but danger is still part of every mission.

On your paper, rewrite this newspaper article, correcting its errors.

Student Rides the Space Shuttle

Jana Parker flew into space on the shuttle endeavor yesterday. A scary ride for most people, but not Jana. Jana says, "Nothing is to scary for me." The shuttle crew will soon send back pictures of Janas adventure in space. Your sure to hear more about this brave girl, she may be on the first spacecraft to reach mars.

Writer's Handbook

The Writer's Handbook is designed to give you more help as well as some great hints for making your writing the best it can be. It uses the Gather, Organize, Write, Elaborate, Clarify, Proofread, and Share categories you have become familiar with during the course of this book. Use the Writer's Handbook any time you have more questions or just need a little extra help.

Table of Contents

Prewriting
Gather

Research

Research is an important part of writing. When you look for information about a topic, you are doing research. It's important to use good sources.

A **source** is anything or anyone with information. **Primary sources** include books or people that are closest to the information. Diaries, journals, and other writings of people who lived during the described events are considered primary sources. **Secondary sources** are books or people who use other books or people to get information. Primary and secondary sources fit into three categories—**printed, electronic,** and **personal**.

Use a variety of primary and secondary sources from different categories when you do research. That way you can make sure the information is accurate and you will have lots of it to choose from. Talk to your teacher about how many sources and what kinds of sources to use for different writing projects.

- **Printed sources** include books, magazines, newspapers, letters, journals and diaries, and reference materials such as encyclopedias and dictionaries.

- **Electronic sources** include the Internet, television, radio, and videos.

- **Personal sources** include people you interview or observe and your own experiences and memories.

When doing research, keep these points in mind:

- When you use sources, be sure they are **credible** ones. Credible means that the source can be trusted to have accurate information. Generally, books, magazines, and reference materials can be considered credible sources. People who are experts in their field and those you know and trust personally are also credible sources.

- Use caution when using Web sites, movies, and television as sources. Many Web sites offer the opinion of the people who created them, not necessarily the facts about a topic. Check several Web sites and some printed sources on the same topic to be sure you are getting "just the facts." Also, Web sites often move or become outdated, so check to see that the ones you are using are still in operation. Finally, make sure you have an adult—a teacher or parent—help you as you do research on the Internet.

- Movies and television offer a lot of information, but it is often difficult to tell if the information is fact, fiction, or someone's opinion. Again, double check with other sources and with an adult to be sure you are getting accurate information.

Printed

Sources

Books, Magazines, Newspapers, Reference Materials, Letters, Journals/Diaries

Where to Find Them

Library, Home, School, Bookstores, Discount Department Stores

How to Use Them

Use headings to find useful information.
Read.
Take notes while reading.

How to Cite Them

(Use punctuation and capitalization as shown.)

Books: Author's Last Name, First Name. Book Title. City: Publishing Company, year.

Magazine Articles: Author's Last Name, First Name. "Title of Article." Title of Magazine, volume number (if there is one), date, month, or season, and year of publication: page number. (If the article is longer than one page, state the first page and the last page of the article with a dash between them.)

Encyclopedias/Dictionaries: Title of Encyclopedia or Dictionary, edition number (ed. __), s.v. "item."
(If you looked up Olympic Games, it would be s.v. "Olympic Games.")

Letters/Diaries/Journals: Mention them in the text as you are writing, rather than citing them later.

Electronic

The Internet,
Television,
Radio,
Videos

The Internet,
Television,
Radio,
Stores, Library

Read Web sites.
Watch the news on television.
Listen to radio programs.
Rent or check out videos.
Take notes as you are reading,
watching, and listening.

Internet: State the Web address of the Web sites you used. Most Web addresses will begin with http:// and end with .com, .net, .org, or .edu.

Films/Videos: Title of Film or Video. City where the production company is located: Production Company Name, year.

Television/Radio: Mention them in the text as you are writing, rather than citing them later.

Personal

Self,
Other People

Home: Parents, Siblings, Grandparents
School: Teachers, Principals, Librarians, Friends, Other Family Members, People in the Community

Listen to people when they tell stories.
Interview people who know something about your topic.
Ask questions.
Take notes.

Personal sources should be mentioned in the text as you are writing.
When interviewing, you can quote the person by enclosing his or her exact words in quotation marks. You can also use phrases such as "according to" to give credit to your source. To give credit to personal sources other than people you interview, simply state where you found the information.

Getting Ideas for Writing

So you have a writing assignment. Now what? Where do you begin? Your mind might be a complete blank right now. You haven't even chosen a topic yet. The early stages of writing are the toughest ones. Good writers use all kinds of techniques to generate new ideas. Here are some ideas to help you get started.

Brainstorming

Brainstorming is a great way to generate lots of ideas in a short amount of time. You can brainstorm alone or with a group of people. All you have to do is say or think one word, and you're off! Here's how it works:

Your assignment is to write an expository essay about an animal. If you're working in a group, the members of the group can brainstorm together. One person starts by saying "animals." The rest of the group can now take turns saying words or phrases that come to mind. Someone says "mammals." Someone else says "reptiles." Another person says "dinosaurs." As this is happening, members of the group should be careful to take turns and give each other time to write down what's being said. As the process continues, you or someone else in the group will probably say something that will become the topic for your essay.

If you're working alone, the process is the same. Think of the initial assignment. Write down words related to the assignment as they come to mind. Eventually, you will find the one word or phrase that will become the topic for your essay. Remember to write down your thoughts as you brainstorm alone, too. That way, if you change your mind, you'll have other choices to work with.

Journaling

A journal is similar to a diary. Both are used to write down personal thoughts. However, diaries are usually used to record daily events and feelings. Journals are generally used to record thoughts, impressions, and responses to events. A journal is a great way to generate ideas for writing.

Writers who use journals keep one with them most of the time. You might want to keep your journal in your book bag or locker and take it home with you after school. That way, when an interesting thought occurs to you, you can write it in your journal no matter where you are. The great thing about journaling is that there's no right or wrong way to do it. It's also great because you don't have to try to keep every good idea in your head. Just write it down and it will always be there, ready to become a topic for writing.

Freewriting

Freewriting is a very unusual method of writing because it has no form. The idea behind freewriting is to write down everything that comes to mind during a specific period of time. Just get out a piece of paper and a pen or pencil, or sit down in front of a computer. For the next few minutes, jot down everything your mind comes up with, even stuff that doesn't make any sense. You don't have to use complete sentences. You don't have to worry about spelling. You don't even have to write words. You can draw, sketch, or doodle as part of freewriting.

When time is up, stop writing (or doodling) and look at what you've got. Read it over a couple of times. You'll be amazed at what you might find. Some of the best ideas for writing show up in the middle of freewriting.

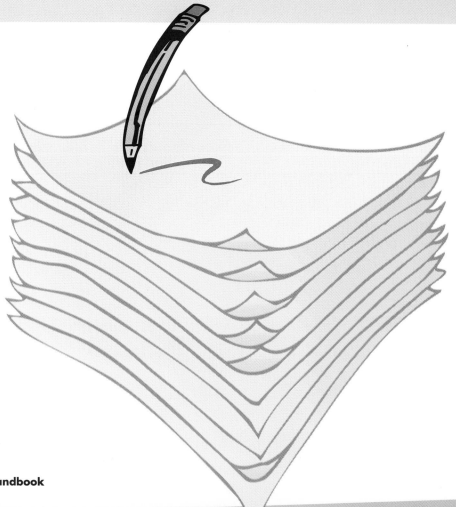

Daydreaming

This one is best done at home. Your teachers probably won't appreciate your daydreaming during class, and daydreaming while crossing the road is downright dangerous.

Try this. When you have some free time at home, get a mug of something good to drink (hot chocolate works great on a cold day). Now find a comfortable spot and—are you ready for this?—don't do anything! At least, don't do anything specific. Daydreaming means letting your mind wander wherever it wants to go. Stare out the window. Watch the goldfish in your fish tank. Listen to the rain. Smell dinner cooking in the kitchen. Think about what you'll be when you're an adult. Something will probably come to mind that will make a great topic for writing.

Here's a tip for how to use daydreaming. As soon as you hit upon a great topic for writing, get up and write down everything you can think of before you forget it. You can organize it later, but it's very important to record it all now. Just like dreams you dream at night, daydreams will disappear quickly, and you don't want to lose all those great ideas.

Reading

Sometimes the easiest way to get ideas for writing is to read. For example, let's say you have been asked to write a piece of narrative historical fiction. You don't know much about history. How do you write about something you don't know? Make use of your library.

Talk to your school librarian or go to the public library and ask for help at the information desk. These people are experts. Tell them you are looking for a few books about history. They will probably ask you some questions such as, "What kind of history are you interested in reading about?" or, "Would you like books about U.S. history or world history?" These questions will help you to make some early decisions about your writing. Once you decide what kind of history you want to read about, pick a few books that are short enough to read quickly, but long enough to have lots of interesting information. Again, people who work at libraries can help you through this process.

As you read about history, you will spot things that interest you. Write down those things. Skip over the stuff you don't find interesting, at least for now. When you are finished reading, look at the notes you took. Do they have anything in common? Do most of them have something to do with specific time periods, people, or things in history? For example, in reading about U.S. history, did you always stop at the sections about inventions because you found that information interesting? Maybe you can focus your writing assignment on an invention or an inventor.

Don't forget to read for your own interest and pleasure. The more you read, the more you'll know. The more you know, the more ideas for writing you will have.

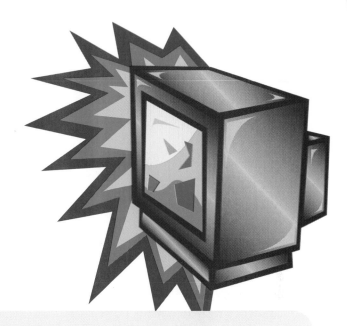

TV/Movies

Great ideas for writing may be as close as your television or movie theater. There are cable channels that run programs specifically about science, technology, history, animals, cooking, music, sports, and just about any other topic you can think of. Public television also has great documentaries and programs about interesting and unusual topics.

Movies can also be good for generating ideas for writing—especially movies that deal with specific topics. Are you a fan of sci-fi movies? You can use your favorite sci-fi movie to come up with ideas for an expository essay about artificial intelligence or a compare-and-contrast report about robots and computers.

Just as you should use caution when using television and movies as sources when you write, be cautious in using them to generate ideas. Make sure you talk to an adult about appropriate and safe choices in movies and television programs.

Interviewing

An interview is the process of asking questions of another person and listening to and recording that person's answers. Interviews make good sources for writing projects, especially if the person you interview is an expert about your topic. Interviews can also be good ways to generate ideas for writing.

Some of the most interesting stories come from people in your community and family. Your parents and grandparents have lived through many events. Sit down with a family member or another trusted adult and ask that person to tell you about a memorable event he or she experienced or an interesting person he or she knew. You'll be amazed at the stories you will hear. Many famous authors say that their stories were inspired by what other people have told them.

As you listen to people's stories, jot down notes. It's safe to say that something the person said during the interview will probably give you a good idea for your own writing project.

Prewriting Organize

Note Taking

As you are doing research for your writing project, you will want to take notes. That way you will have the most important information in small pieces that you can use easily. However, taking notes can be tricky, especially for the beginner. Here are some things to keep in mind:

- Keep your notes short. You don't have to use complete sentences, as long as you include the important information.

- Make sure your handwriting is legible. If you scribble, you may not be able to read your own notes later.

- Use note cards. That way you can arrange your notes without having to rewrite them. Try using different colors of note cards to help you organize your notes.

- When listening to a speaker and taking notes, don't try to write down what the speaker is saying "word for word." Just make sure you get the important stuff.

- When you are interviewing, however, you will want to get the exact words down on paper. In this case, ask the speaker to repeat what he or she said, so you can write the quote. If it's possible, use a tape recorder during the interview, so you can listen to the quote as often as you need to. Just make sure you get the speaker's permission to record the interview.

- It's important to write down the source of your information on your note cards as you are taking notes. That way you can cite or credit your sources easily.

Graphic Organizers

A graphic organizer is a tool that helps writers put information in order before they start a draft. Graphic organizers include storyboards, sequence chains, spider maps, network trees, support patterns, attribute charts, cause-and-effect chains, story maps, pros-and-cons charts, 5 W's charts, order-of-importance organizers, main idea tables, Venn diagrams, and outlines. When you do other writing projects, you'll want to continue to use them to help you keep track of information. What kind of graphic organizers you use depends on what kind of writing project you have. Check back with this book to see what kind of graphic organizer works best for different writing projects.

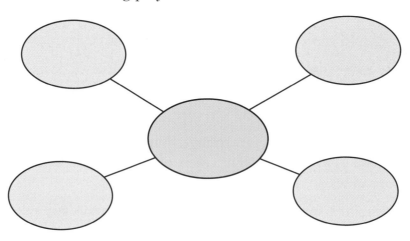

Outlining

There are many ways to organize information. One very useful organizer that you have used is an outline. The outline helps you put your information in the order it will appear in your writing. The outline can be divided into several basic pieces—the introduction, the body, and the conclusion—just like a basic essay. Every letter and number in the outline stands for something in your essay. Words or phrases that are designated with Roman numerals represent entire chunks of an essay. Words or phrases that are designated with capital letters represent paragraphs which support a main statement or idea. Words or phrases that are designated with regular numbers represent specific details. Here's a basic outline.

I. Introduction

gets audience's attention → **A. Lead**

moves closer to the main idea → **B. Related statement**

C. Transitional statement

states main idea of essay

introduce the essay to the audience

II. Body

states main idea of paragraph → **A. First main idea**

1. First supporting detail
2. Second supporting detail
3. Third supporting detail

support, explain, and give more information about main idea of essay

B. Second main idea

1. First supporting detail
2. Second supporting detail
3. Third supporting detail

same as paragraph A

C. Third main idea

1. First supporting detail
2. Second supporting detail
3. Third supporting detail

same as paragraphs A and B

III. Conclusion

restates main ideas of body paragraphs → **A. Brief summary of main ideas**

begins to wrap up essay → **B. Other related statement**

ends the essay → **C. Closing statement**

wrap up essay

Writing Paragraphs

A paragraph is a group of related sentences. The main idea of a paragraph is usually in the first sentence, called the **topic sentence**. The rest of the sentences in a paragraph give more information about the topic sentence. Start with the idea you want your audience to know. This will become the topic sentence for your paragraph. For example, let's say your essay is an expository piece about horses. You have gathered information about horses and made a web to put your information in order.

Your web may look something like this:

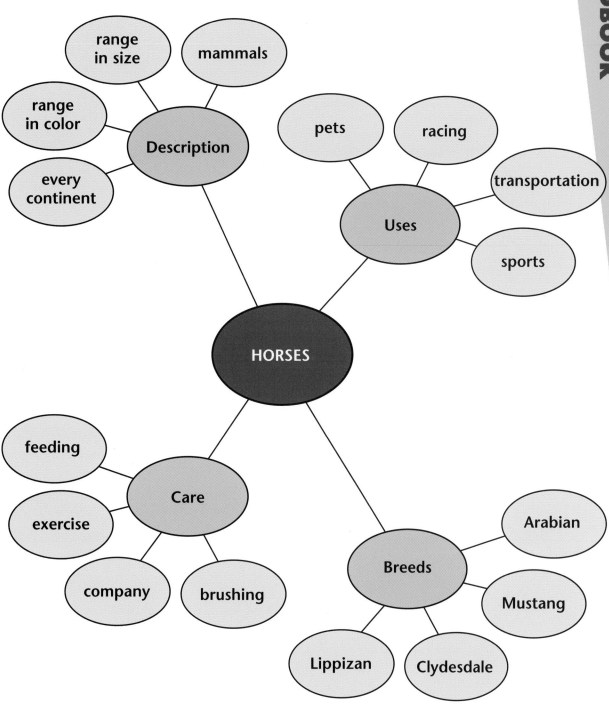

Take one part of your web—Breeds. Write it as a sentence. You might come up with this:

There are many different kinds, or breeds, of horses.

This is now your topic sentence. Now it's time to tell your audience more information about the main idea. If you have gathered information about horses, you might have these facts.

1. Arabian horses were prized by Bedouin tribes in the desert for their speed, beauty, and intelligence.
2. The Mustang is a well-known breed in North America and descends from Spanish horses.
3. The Clydesdale is native to Scotland and is one of the largest breeds.
4. The Lippizan horses were bred for the royal family of Spain, who valued them for their dazzling white coats, graceful appearance, and gentleness.

When you combine your topic sentence with these supporting sentences, you have a paragraph.

There are many different kinds, or breeds, of horses. Arabian horses were prized by Bedouin tribes in the desert for their speed, beauty, and intelligence. The Mustang is a well-known breed in North America and descends from Spanish horses. The Clydesdale is native to Scotland and is one of the largest breeds. The Lippizan horses were bred for the royal family of Spain, who valued them for their dazzling white coats, graceful appearance, and gentleness.

Following the same steps for the other three parts of your web will give you three more paragraphs. Put these together, and you will have the body of a well-organized essay. All you need now is an introduction and a conclusion. For tips about writing good introductions and conclusions see "Writing a Five-Paragraph Essay" on page HB20.

Writing a Five-Paragraph Essay

An essay is a piece of nonfiction writing about one topic. In grades 5 and 6, you practice writing a descriptive essay, a compare-and-contrast essay, a cause-and-effect essay, and a persuasive essay. Essays are made up of three basic parts—the introduction, the body, and the conclusion.

Write the body of your essay first. It doesn't matter that you don't have an introduction yet. It's very difficult to write a good introduction until you have written the body. Imagine trying to introduce a person you don't know to an audience. What would you say? That's kind of what it's like to try writing an introduction first. You don't know your essay yet. Write the body first and then you'll know what to say in your introduction.

Body

The body of your essay is where you explain, describe, prove, and give information about your main idea. Look at your graphic organizer. There's a good chance that you already have the makings of several good paragraphs.

Let's pretend you're writing a descriptive essay on your favorite vacation spot—the beach. After gathering and organizing your information, you may have three main points in your graphic organizer—how it looks, how it feels, and how it sounds. Look at the web on page HB21.

To move from one paragraph to the next, use a trick good writers know. It's called a "signal word." There's a list of these words on page HB41.

Once you have written all the paragraphs of the body of your essay, it's time to write the introduction and the conclusion.

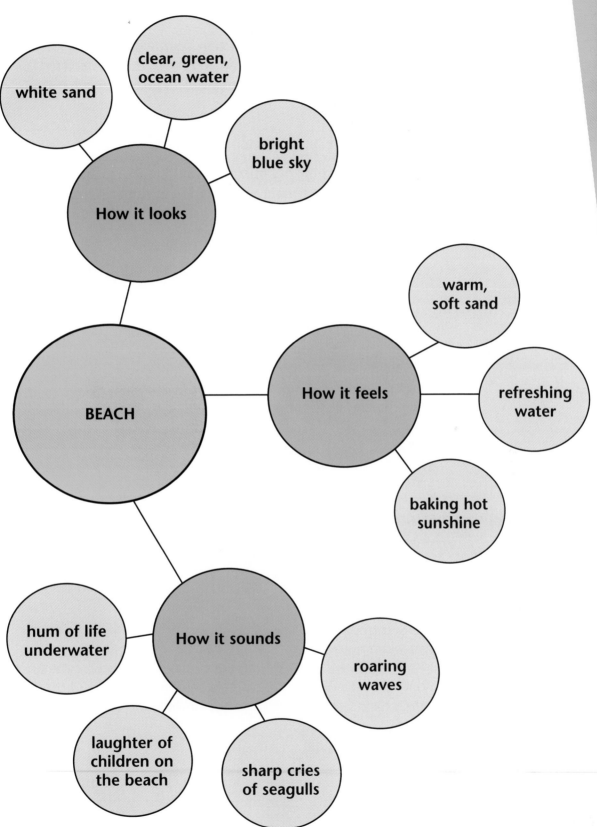

white sand

clear, green, ocean water

bright blue sky

How it looks

BEACH

How it feels

warm, soft sand

refreshing water

baking hot sunshine

How it sounds

hum of life underwater

roaring waves

laughter of children on the beach

sharp cries of seagulls

Introduction

The introduction is the first part of the essay that your audience will read or hear. You want it to get their attention and make them interested enough to keep reading or listening. You don't want to give away what's in the essay.

The Upside-Down Pyramid

If your introduction were a graphic organizer, it would look like an upside-down pyramid with more general information at the beginning and more specific information at the end. Let's write an introduction for our descriptive essay about the beach.

The first sentence of your introduction should say something true but general about your topic.

There are many great places to go on vacation.

This sentence gives some examples of vacation spots. It's still pretty general, but it gets closer to the main idea.

Amusement parks, campgrounds, and cities are some good choices for vacation spots.

This sentence should be the main idea of your essay.

For the sights, the sounds, and feeling good, nothing beats my favorite vacation spot—the beach.

Here's the complete introduction:

There are many great places to go on vacation. Amusement parks, campgrounds, and cities are some good choices for vacation spots. For the sights, the sounds, and feeling good, nothing beats my favorite vacation spot—the beach.

Remember—start with something general and true. Then say something a little more specific. Finish with the main idea of the essay. Now your introduction is complete.

Conclusion

The conclusion of an essay does two things. It restates the main idea of the essay, and it wraps up the essay. Restating the main idea is important. You want to make sure your audience remembers what the essay was about. Wrapping things up helps the audience feel that they have read a complete work and that nothing is missing.

The Right-Side-Up Pyramid

If the introduction of your essay looks like an upside-down pyramid, the conclusion looks like a pyramid right-side-up with more specific information at the beginning and more general information at the end. Here's how:

The first sentence of the conclusion should restate the main idea.

The beach is an amazing place to go on vacation if you want to see beautiful things, hear interesting and fun sounds, and feel great.

The next sentence should say something a little more general but still stay on the main idea.

It's a good idea to visit different and interesting places on vacation.

The final sentence should wrap things up and finish the essay. It should be very general.

Beaches all over the world offer a wonderful way to relax and enjoy your vacation.

When you put your conclusion together, it will look like this:

The beach is an amazing place to go on vacation if you want to see beautiful things, hear interesting and fun sounds, and feel great. It's a good idea to visit different and interesting places on vacation. Beaches all over the world offer a wonderful way to relax and enjoy your vacation.

Writing Poetry

Poetry is different from other forms of writing. Some poems are written in lines and stanzas and follow a rhyme or rhythm. Some poems are simply words or phrases with no rhyme. Most poems are full of imagery or word pictures. Whatever form a poem takes, it's one of the most creative forms of writing.

When you start to write a poem, the first thing to do is to pick a subject. It's a good idea to pick a subject that you know something about or a subject that means a lot to you. Next you should try to write down interesting ideas about your subject. You can write down your ideas however you like.

Then it is time to write your first draft. Once again, you can use any form you like to write your poem. Be sure to use plenty of descriptive words, or words that describe sounds, smells, tastes, and how things look and feel. As you begin to write, your poem might already be taking on its own form.

Revising is an important part of all writing, including writing poetry. You'll probably revise your poem many times. You might want to try changing the form of your poem. Once it's written, you may think it would be better stated in rhyme. You may think your poem is better if it doesn't rhyme. Just make sure your poem's message and ideas are clear to your readers.

Once you have written your final version, read it over to yourself. Then read it out loud. You may find more areas to improve.

Types of Poetry

Ballad: A ballad tells a story. Ballads are usually written as quatrains (four-line stanzas). Often, the first and third lines have four accented syllables; the second and fourth have three.

Blank Verse: Blank verse poems do not rhyme, but they have meter. Beginning with the second syllable of a line, every other syllable is accented.

Epic: An epic is a long poem that tells a story. The story describes adventures of heroes.

Free Verse: Free verse poems do not rhyme and do not have meter.

Haiku: Haiku is a form of poetry developed in Japan. The words of a haiku poem represent nature. A haiku is three lines in length. The first line is five syllables; the second is seven syllables; and the third is five syllables in length.

Limerick: A limerick is a funny poem that has five lines. Lines one, two, and five rhyme and have three stressed syllables. Lines three and four rhyme and have two stressed syllables.

Lyric: A lyric is a short poem that expresses personal feeling.

Ode: An ode is a long lyric. It expresses deeper feelings and uses poetic devices and imagery.

Sonnet: A sonnet is a fourteen-line poem that expresses personal feeling. Each line in a sonnet is ten syllables in length; every other syllable is stressed, beginning with the second syllable.

Poetry Terms

Alliteration: Alliteration is the repeating of the beginning consonant sounds:

> cute, cuddly, calico cats

End Rhyme: End rhyme refers to the rhyming words at the ends of two or more lines of poetry:

> Her favorite pastime was to take a **hike**.
> His first choice was to ride a **bike**.

Foot: A foot is one unit of meter.

Meter: Meter is the pattern of accented and unaccented syllables in the lines of a traditional poem.

Onomatopoeia: Onomatopoeia is the use of a word whose sound makes you think of its meaning. Here are some examples:

> bang, beep, buzz, clang, swish, thump, zoom

Quatrain: A quatrain is a four-line stanza:

> At night she looks up at the stars
> And thinks of what might be.
> By day she works and studies so
> To someday live her dreams.

Stanza: A stanza is a section in a poem named for the number of lines it contains.

Verse: Verse is a name for a line of traditional poetry.

Revising
Elaborate and Clarify

Thesaurus

When it comes to saying things in different, more interesting ways, the thesaurus is one of the best friends a writer can have.

A thesaurus is a reference book that lists the *synonyms* (words that have the same or similar meaning) of words, and the *antonyms* (words that have the opposite meaning) of words.

Many times writers get stuck using the same words over and over. It's difficult to think of new and more colorful words. The next time you are writing, ask yourself, "Have I used a word too many times? Is there a better way to say this?" Chances are, the answer will be yes. That's where a thesaurus can help.

For example, let's say you are writing a descriptive essay about a place, and you have picked a beach where you vacationed last summer. You have written that the ocean was **beautiful**. You have said that the sky was a **beautiful** shade of blue. You have stated that the tropical plants were **beautiful**. Do you see a pattern yet?

All those things were beautiful, but there are more colorful words you can use. Maybe the ocean is **stunning** or **spectacular**. The sky might be a **lovely** or even an **exquisite** shade of blue. And how about those tropical plants? Are they **extravagant, magnificent,** or **dramatic** in their beauty? Use rich words and your writing becomes truly **fabulous**.

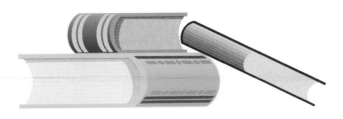

Dictionary

One of the most helpful tools for writers is the dictionary. Just think of it! Every word you could possibly need is in there. Until now, you might have used your dictionary only to look up the spellings of difficult words. That's important because good spelling makes writing clearer, but it's not the only information in a dictionary.

Your dictionary contains valuable information, such as the history of words, a guide for pronunciation, foreign words and phrases, the names of historical people, the names of places in the world, and lots of other interesting things. Some dictionaries even contain the Declaration of Independence and the Constitution of the United States! The next time you are looking for more than just the spelling of a word, try your dictionary.

Web Sites

With the help of an adult, try these Web sites for even more help in building your vocabulary and making your writing richer and clearer.

http://www.writetools.com
This is a one-stop Web site for writers. It contains links to reference materials, almanacs, calendars, historical documents, government resources, grammar and style guides, and all kinds of other tools for writing and editing.

http://www.bartleby.com
This Web site has links to several on-line dictionaries, encyclopedias, thesauri, and many other useful and interesting sources. It also contains links to on-line fiction and nonfiction books. It's like having a library of your own.

Capitalization

Capitalize:

- the first word in a sentence.
- all proper nouns, including people's names and the names of particular places.
- titles of respect.
- family titles used just before people's names and titles of respect that are part of names.
- initials of names.
- place names.
- proper adjectives, adjectives that are made from proper nouns.
- the months of the year and the days of the week.
- important words in the names of organizations.
- important words in the names of holidays.
- the first word in the greeting or closing of a letter.
- the word *I*.
- the first, last, and most important words in a title. Be sure to capitalize all verbs including *is* and *was*.
- the first word in a direct quotation.

Sentence Structure

The Sentence

A sentence is a group of words that tells a complete thought.
A sentence has two parts: a **subject** and a **predicate**.

- The complete subject tells who or what.
  A famous artist painted the picture.

- The complete predicate tells what happened.
  A famous artist **painted the picture**.

Subject

The **subject** of a sentence tells whom or what the sentence is about.

- The **complete** subject includes all the words that name and tell about the subject.

  A **famous artist** painted the picture.

- The **simple** subject is the most important noun or pronoun in the complete subject.

  A famous **artist** painted the picture.

- A sentence can have one subject.

  Jessica walked home.

- A sentence can have a **compound** subject, two or more subjects that share the same predicate.

  Jessica and Joan walked home.

Predicate

The **predicate** of a sentence tells what happened.
The **complete** predicate includes a verb and all the words that tell what happened.

- A **complete** predicate can tell what the subject of the sentence did. This kind of predicate includes an action verb.

  A famous artist **painted the picture**.

- A complete predicate can also tell more about the subject. This kind of predicate includes a **linking verb**.

  The coat **was** red wool.

- A **predicate noun** follows a linking verb and renames the subject.

  The garment was **a coat**.

- A **predicate adjective** follows a linking verb and describes the subject.

  The coat was **red**.

- A **compound** predicate is two or more predicates that share the same subject. Compound predicates are often joined by the conjunction *and* or *or*.

  James **ran** across the deck and **jumped** into the pool.

- The **simple** predicate is the most important word or words in the complete predicate. The simple predicate is always a verb.

  A famous artist **painted** the picture.

Simple, Compound, and Complex Sentences

- A **simple** sentence tells one complete thought.

  A famous artist painted the picture.

- A **compound** sentence is made up of two simple sentences joined by a comma and a conjunction *(and, or, but)*. The two simple sentences in a compound sentence can also be joined by a semicolon. Two simple sentences can go together to make one compound sentence if the ideas in the simple sentences are related.

  Tony cut out the letters, **and** Shanna glued them to the poster.

- A **complex** sentence is made up of one **independent clause** (or simple sentence), and at least one **dependent clause**. A **dependent clause** is a group of words that has a subject and a predicate but cannot stand on its own.

  Dependent Clause: while Shanna glued them to the poster
  Independent Clause: Tony cut out the letters
  Complex Sentence: Tony cut out the letters, while Shanna glued them to the poster.

Subject-Verb Agreement

- The subject and its verb must agree in number.

  One **part** of speech **is** a noun.
  (*Part* is singular; it requires the verb *is*.)

  The **sweatshirts** on the rack **were** on sale.
  (*Sweatshirts* is plural; it requires the verb *were*.)

- Sometimes a **helping verb** is needed to help the main verb show action. A helping verb comes before a main verb.

  Joe **has watched** the team practice.

- An **action verb** shows action in a sentence.

  A penguin **waddles** and **slides** on the ice.

- A **linking verb** does not show action. It connects the subject of a sentence to a word or words in the predicate that tell about the subject. Linking verbs include *am, is, are, was,* and *were. Seem* and *become* are linking verbs, too.

  The coat **is** red wool.
  This milk **seems** sour.

Abbreviations

Abbreviations are shortened forms of words. Many abbreviations begin with a capital letter and end with a period.

Abbreviate:

- titles of address and titles of respect.
    - Mister (Mr. Robert Sing)
    - Mistress (Mrs. Amy Walters)
    - Doctor (Dr. Donna Rodrigues)

- words used in addresses.
    - Street (St.)
    - Avenue (Ave.)
    - Route (Rt.)
    - Boulevard (Blvd.)
    - Road (Rd.)

- certain words in the names of businesses.
    - Incorporated (Inc.)
    - Corporation (Corp.)
    - Limited (Ltd.)

- days of the week when you take notes.
    - Sunday (Sun.)
    - Monday (Mon.)
    - Tuesday (Tues.)
    - Wednesday (Wed.)
    - Thursday (Thurs.)
    - Friday (Fri.)
    - Saturday (Sat.)

- most months of the year.
    - January (Jan.)
    - February (Feb.)
    - March (Mar.)
    - April (Apr.)
    - August (Aug.)
    - September (Sept.)
    - October (Oct.)
    - November (Nov.)
    - December (Dec.)
    - (May, June, and July do not have abbreviated forms.)

- directions.
    - North (N)
    - East (E)
    - South (S)
    - West (W)

Quotation Marks

Quotation marks are used to separate a speaker's exact words from the rest of the sentence. Begin a **direct quotation** with a capital letter. Use a comma to separate the direct quotation from the speaker's name. When a direct quotation comes at the end of a sentence, put the end mark inside the last quotation mark. When writing a conversation, begin a new paragraph with each change of speaker. For example:

Tim said, "My homework is done." He was hoping to go rollerblading before dinner.

"You can go," his mom answered. "Just be back before dinnertime."

End Marks

Every sentence must end with a **period,** an **exclamation point,** or a **question mark.**

- Use a **period** at the end of a statement (declarative sentence) or a command (imperative sentence).
  Statement: The sky is blue.
  Command: Please come here.

- Use an **exclamation point** at the end of a firm command (imperative sentence)
  Shut the door!

  or at the end of a sentence that shows great feeling or excitement (exclamatory sentence)
  It's hot!

- Use a **question mark** at the end of an asking sentence (interrogative sentence).
  Is it raining?

Commas

Use a **comma:**

- after an introductory word in a sentence.
  Wow, you're here.

- to separate items in a series. Put the last comma before *and* or *or*.
  Jessica bought paper, pens, and a pencil.

- when speaking directly to a person.
  Alan, take your seat.

- to separate a direct quotation from the speaker's name.
  Tim said, "My homework is done."

- with the conjunctions *and, or,* or *but* when combining independent clauses in a compound sentence.
  He could play soccer, or he could run track.

Parts of Speech

Nouns

- A **singular noun** names one person, place, thing, or idea.
  boy   watch   cat

- A **plural noun** names more than one person, place, thing or idea.
  To make most singular nouns plural, add -*s*.
  boys   cats

- For nouns ending in *sh, ch, x,* or *z*, add -*es* to make the word plural.
  watch/watches   box/boxes

- For nouns ending in a consonant and *y*, change the *y* to *i* and add -*es*.
  pony/ponies   story/stories

- For many nouns that end in *f* or *fe*, replace *f* or *fe* with *ves* to make the noun plural.
  hoof/hooves   shelf/shelves

- Some words change spelling when the plural is formed.
  man/men   child/children

- Some words have the same singular and plural form.
  deer/deer   fish/fish

Possessive Nouns

A **possessive noun** shows ownership.

- To make a singular noun possessive, add an apostrophe and -*s*.

    boy/boy's   cat/cat's   watch/watch's

- When a singular noun ends in *s*, add an apostrophe and -*s*.
  dress/dress's   class/class's

- To make a plural noun that ends in *s* possessive, add an apostrophe.
  boys/boys'   cats/cats'   watches/watches'

- When a plural noun does not end in *s*, add an apostrophe and -*s* to show possession.
  women/women's   children/children's

Verbs

Verbs can tell about the present, the past, or the future.

- The **present tense** is used to show that something happens regularly or is true now.

    Add -*s* to most verbs to show present tense when the subject is *he, she, it,* or a singular noun.

        He walks to school.

    Add -*es* to verbs ending in *s, ch, sh, x,* or *z*.
        Joe watches the team practice.

    Do not add -*s* or -*es* if the subject is a plural noun or *I, you, we,* or *they*.
        I want to go to the park.

    Change *y* to *i* and add -*es* to form some present tense verbs.
        Sam hurries to school.

- The **past tense** shows past action. Add *-ed* to most verbs to form the past tense.

    climb/climbed　　　watch/watched　　　show/showed

- Past tense verbs that do not add *-ed* are called **irregular verbs**.

Present	Past	Past Participle (with *have, has,* or *had*)
bring	brought	brought
go	went	gone
grow	grew	grown
know	knew	known
take	took	taken

- The **future tense** indicates future action. Use the helping verb *will* to form the future tense.

    Joe will watch the team practice.

- The **present perfect tense** shows action that began in the past and may still be happening. To form the present perfect tense, add the helping verb *has* or *have* to the past participle of a verb.

    Joe has watched the team practice.

Pronouns

A **pronoun** can replace a **noun** naming a person, place, thing, or idea. Personal pronouns include *I, me, you, we, us, he, she, it, they,* and *them.*

- A **subject** pronoun takes the place of the subject of a sentence. Subject pronouns are said to be in the **subjective case**. Do not use both the pronoun and the noun it replaces together.

    Incorrect: Marla she answered the question.
    Correct: Marla answered the question.

- An **object** pronoun replaces a noun that is the object of a verb or preposition. Object pronouns are said to be in the **objective case**.

  Rosco came with **us**.

- Use a **subject** pronoun as part of a **compound subject**. Use an **object** pronoun as part of a **compound object**. To test whether a pronoun is correct, say the sentence *without* the other part of a compound subject or object.

  Incorrect: Rosco and **him** came with Jessica and **we**.
  Correct: Rosco and **he** came with Jessica and **us**.

- An **antecedent** is the word or phrase a pronoun refers to. The antecedent always includes a noun.

  Joan cleaned **her** room.

- A pronoun must match its antecedent. An antecedent and pronoun agree when they have the same **number** (singular or plural) and **gender** (male or female).

- **Possessive** pronouns show ownership. The words *my, your, his, her, its, their,* and *our* are possessive pronouns.

- The **interrogative** pronouns *who, what,* and *which* are used to ask questions.

  Who opened the window?

- *This, that, these,* and *those* can be used as **demonstrative** pronouns. Use *this* and *these* to talk about one or more things that are nearby. Use *that* and *those* to talk about one or more things that are far away.

  This is interesting.
  That is his new car.
  Those are my favorite.

Prepositions

A **preposition** shows a relationship between a word in a sentence and a noun or pronoun that follows the preposition. Prepositions help tell *when, where, what kind, how,* or *how much.*

Common Prepositions

aboard	behind	from	throughout
about	below	in	to
above	beneath	into	toward
across	beside	like	under
after	between	near	underneath
against	beyond	of	until
along	but (except)	off	unto
amid	by	on	up
among	down	over	upon
around	during	past	with
at	except	since	within
before	for	through	without

Conjunctions

The words *and, or,* and *but* are **coordinating conjunctions**.

- Coordinating conjunctions may be used to join words within a sentence.
    Jessica bought paper, pens, **and** a pencil.

- A comma and a coordinating conjunction can be used to join two or more simple sentences.
    Tony cut out the letters, **and** Shanna glued them to the poster.

Negatives

A negative word says "no" or "not."

- Often negatives are in the form of contractions.
  isn't, doesn't, haven't

- It is not correct to use two negatives to refer to the same thing.
  Incorrect: Tina **hasn't never** seen the ocean.
  Correct: Tina **hasn't ever** seen the ocean.

Homophones

Homophones are words that sound alike but have different spellings and meanings.

- Here is a list of some homophones often confused in writing.

are	**Are** is a form of the verb *be*.
our	**Our** is a possessive noun.
hour	An **hour** is sixty minutes.
its	**Its** is a possessive pronoun.
it's	**It's** is a contraction of the words *it is*.
there	**There** means "in that place." It can also be used as an introductory word.
their	**Their** is a possessive pronoun. It shows something belongs to more than one person or thing.
they're	**They're** is a contraction made from the words *they are*.
two	**Two** is a number.
to	**To** means "toward."
too	**Too** means "also." **Too** can mean "more than enough."
your	**Your** is a possessive pronoun.
you're	**You're** is a contraction made from the words *you are*.
whose	**Whose** is a possessive pronoun.
who's	**Who's** is a contraction made from the words *who* and *is* or *who* and *has*.

ate	**Ate** is a form of the verb *eat*.
eight	**Eight** is a number word.
principal	A **principal** is a person with authority.
principle	A **principle** is a general rule or code of behavior.
waist	The **waist** is the middle part of the body.
waste	To **waste** something is to use it in a careless way.
aloud	**Aloud** means out loud, or able to be heard.
allowed	**Allowed** is a form of the verb *allow*.

Signal Words

Signal words help writers move from one idea to another. Here is a list of some common signal words.

Time-Order Signal Words

after	third	later	as soon as
before	till	immediately	when
during	until	finally	then
first	meanwhile	soon	next
second			

Comparison/Contrast Signal Words

in the same way	likewise	as	also
similarly	like	as well	
but	however	otherwise	yet
still	even though	although	on the other hand

Concluding or Summarizing Signal Words

as a result	finally	in conclusion	to sum up
therefore	lastly	in summary	all in all

Writing a Letter

Friendly Letters

A friendly letter is an informal letter written to a friend or family member. In a friendly letter, you might send a message, invite someone to a party, or thank someone for a gift. A friendly letter has five parts:

- The **heading** gives your address and the date.
- The **greeting** includes the name of the person you are writing to. It begins with a capital letter and ends with a comma.
- The **body** of the letter gives your message.
- The **closing** is a friendly or polite way to say good-bye. It begins with a capital letter and ends with a comma.
- The **signature** is your name.

Business Letters

A business letter is a formal letter. You would write a business letter to a company, an employer, a newspaper, or any person you do not know well. A business letter looks a lot like a friendly letter, but a business letter includes the name and address of the business you are writing to. The greeting of a business letter begins with a capital letter and ends with a **colon (:)**.

Addressing Letters

The envelope below shows how to address a letter. A friendly letter and a business letter are addressed the same way.

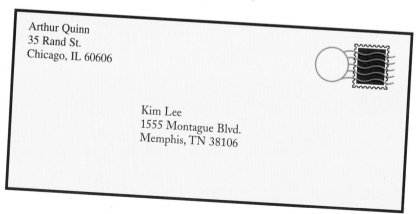

Arthur Quinn
35 Rand St.
Chicago, IL 60606

Kim Lee
1555 Montague Blvd.
Memphis, TN 38106

Publishing
Share

This is the last step of the writing process. You have gathered and organized information. You have drafted, revised, and edited your writing. Your project is completed. Here are some tips for publishing your work.

Ways to Publish

There are lots of ways to publish your work. Keep your audience in mind as you choose different publishing methods. Your teacher might ask you to publish your work by writing your final draft on a clean piece of paper, with a title and your name at the top. You might try one of the publishing methods from this book, like an author's circle or a letter with an addressed envelope. It all depends on who is going to read or listen to your work.

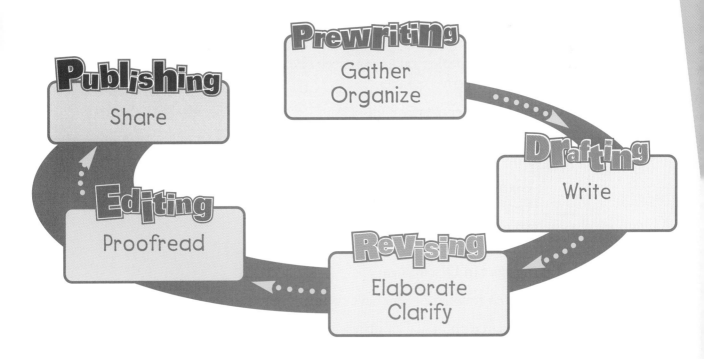

Publishing
Share

Prewriting
Gather
Organize

Drafting
Write

Revising
Elaborate
Clarify

Editing
Proofread

Listening, Speaking, and Thinking Skills

Listening

These tips will help you be a good listener:

- Listen carefully when others are speaking.

- Keep in mind your reason for listening. Are you listening to learn about a topic? To be entertained? To get directions? Decide what you should get out of the listening experience.

- Look directly at the speaker. Doing this will help you concentrate on what he or she has to say.

- Do not interrupt the speaker or talk to others while the speaker is talking.

- Ask questions when the speaker is finished talking if there is anything you did not understand.

Speaking

Being a good speaker takes practice. These guidelines can help you become an effective speaker.

Giving Oral Reports

- Be prepared. Know exactly what you are going to talk about and how long you will speak. Have your notes in front of you.

- Speak slowly and clearly. Speak loudly enough so everyone can hear you.

- Look at your audience.

Taking Part in Discussions

- Listen to what others have to say.

- Disagree politely. Let others in the group know you respect their points of view.

- Try not to interrupt others. Everyone should have a chance to speak.

Thinking

Writers use a variety of thinking skills as they work through the writing process. These skills include **logic, analyzing, setting goals, creativity, and problem solving**. As you write, keep these skills in mind and try to put them to use as much as possible.

- **Logic** Writers use logic to support a point of view by using reasoning, facts, and examples.

- **Analyzing** Analyzing is a thinking skill that requires the writer to think about and examine the information learned about a topic. Once the information is examined, a general conclusion or more meaningful understanding can be made about the topic.

- **Setting Goals** When setting goals, writers must think about deadlines (when the assignment is due; how much time there is for prewriting, drafting, revising, editing, and publishing), the objective of the writing assignment, and the amount of research required.

- **Creativity** Using creativity means using the imagination. Writers let their minds wonder about many different ways to tackle an assignment before finally settling on one. It is often necessary to start an assignment, stop, try it a different way, stop again, and maybe even go back to the original idea. Thinking creatively and openly allows the writer to examine many options.

- **Problem Solving** Learning to problem solve helps writers make decisions about the writing assignment and helps them use facts and opinions correctly. Strategies for problem solving include: naming the problem; thinking of everything about the problem; thinking of ways to solve the problem; choosing the best plan to solve the problem and trying it out; and analyzing the result.